DARE TO LIVE

TRUST YOURSELF

DIANE CARTER

FIRST PUBLISHED IN 2009

National Library of Australia Cataloguing-in-Publication.

Carter, Diane

Dare to Live Trust Yourself.

ISBN: 9780980726800 - 2nd Edition - Paperback

ISBN: 9781621120735 - ebook

Editor: Susanne Hoepfner, Ewingar Document & Office Services

Cover & text design: type*n*graphics

CONTENTS

Preface vii

PART ONE
DARE TO!

1. Dare to survive 3
2. Dare to laugh 10
3. Dare to fall in love 16
4. Dare to perceive differently 23
5. Dare to get your priorities right 27
6. Dare to look back with no regrets 30
7. Dare to achieve the impossible 35
8. Dare to follow your dreams 37
9. Dare to persist 41
10. Dare to cope with death 44
11. Dare to make the best of everything 51
12. Dare to enjoy relationships 55
13. Dare to mature 59

PART TWO
THEY DARED!

Introduction 65

JULIE DARED TO SURVIVE A CAR ACCIDENT 67
By Julie Christie Scott

STEVEN DARED TO TURN HIS LIFE AROUND 75
By Steven Scharenguivel

SIMONE DARED TO SURVIVE CANCER 86
By Simone Riddell

STACEY DARED TO COPE DIFFERENTLY 94
By Stacey Huish

TRACY DARED TO FULFILL A PROMISE 103
By Tracy Eather

BRIAN DARED TO CLIMB MOUNTAINS 111
By Brian Huack

JALEESA – SURVIVES AND THRIVES – SHE JUST LIVES! 116
By Jaleesa Pon

They dared 121

About the Author 123

This book is dedicated to

My younger daughter, Jenna Gilbert,
A beautiful, caring and loving person
who embraces life fully.

And to the memory of my elder daughter, Alison Menage,
A true, free spirit who lived life to the full.
I am so proud of you both.

And to Tony Carter, My Soul Mate,
Who loves me, encourages me and believes in me.

Thank you for being part of my life.
I love you all.

PREFACE

PREFACE

Life is one great adventure and you have it in the power of your mind to make it the greatest adventure of all time. You only have one life, so it is up to you to make it the best you can. My life has been stupendous and it just seems to keep getting better and better, it is only now that I realize why. It's because I have always had *Mindset Energy* - the will and the determination to get up and go.

Our energy determines how we feel, how we think and how we act.

These three together make up our attitude. By choosing a positive attitude, you create positive waves of energy, which attract more of the same so your positive choice sets you on the path to a fulfilling, happy and prosperous life.

It is totally your choice that determines your life, so you need to be very aware of how you react or respond to the situations you find yourself in. 'Dare to Live' will help you to realise that you do have choices and you can lead a successful and fulfilling life. Its powerful stories will show you how to make the best choices possible to be able to reach your goals and make your dreams come true.

PART ONE
DARE TO!

CHAPTER ONE
DARE TO SURVIVE

I believe that we all just take life for granted until something happens to bring us up short and make us take stock of what we have in life. For me, it all started with a hyena... But NO! Actually it didn't. It started before that.

Do you ever have times when your own words come back to you? Each term, as the Head of a private, primary school in the farming town of Chipinge on the south-eastern border of Zimbabwe, I chose a keyword and based my assemblies around this word.

In the middle term of 2003, I chose the word *Challenges*, and in the 3rd term - *Attitude*. The stories, homilies, quotations, etc that I spoke about to the children certainly set me up for my start to 2004.

My daughter, Jenna had phoned me.

"Mom, would you and Jim like to come on a fishing trip on the River for New Year?" The river was the Zambesi River on the border between Zimbabwe and Zambia. My husband, Jim, opted not to join the party as he reckoned he had done enough camping in his lifetime. I phoned to tell Jenna that I'd love to go but that Jim wouldn't. She laughed and said that her Dad, my first husband, Geoff, was going to come but his wife, Avril, wouldn't, for exactly the same reason as Jim, and asked if Jim would mind me going if Geoff was on his own. Well, no one minded, so that was okay.

About fourteen of us met up in Harare at sun-up, loaded the vehicles with all our camping gear, fishing rods, beer and wine, food and other essentials. In a wonderful, light-hearted holiday spirit, we all set out in convoy for Mongwe, thirty kilometres downstream from Chirundu, on the banks of the mighty Zambezi River, which forms the boundary between Zimbabwe and Zambia, a really unique and special area of Zimbabwe – in fact, the whole of the Zambezi Valley is spectacular. The first part of the journey to Makuti took a few hours on good tar roads. We then wound our way downwards into the Zambesi Valley, the tar becoming narrower, the heat increasing, until we turned off the road and travelled down an indistinct, winding dirt track through the bush. As it was the rainy season, occasionally one of the vehicles would flounder in the mud, as we crossed rivers and elephant tracks, and it would have to be pulled out by one of the 4X4s.

The convoy eventually arrived at our destination by mid-afternoon, an abandoned fishing camp that was being *resuscitated* by my son-in-law, Trevor, and a few of his friends, who had gone into partnership in the venture. There were quite a few of these camps along the Zambezi that had previously been owned by white Zimbabweans. The owners had been chased away by 'freedom fighters' and National Parks had taken over the camps. Now seriously neglected, National Parks were inviting these same white Zimbos back to the camps to try and put them right again and encourage tourism. They could see how beautiful the developments on the Zambian side of the river were and how popular they were for holidays and fishing trips and how tourists were pouring into the area across the river.

This particular camp was set right on the banks of the river on quite a steep slope. A fairly basic ablution block was perched on the top with spectacular views of the river, which you could enjoy whilst taking a shower. Halfway down the slope was a dilapidated double storey stone and thatch building. Upstairs was a large half-walled sleeping area. Downstairs was a basic kitchen and sitting and dining area. This was in a really bad state of repair and needed a good clean, so we all set about with brooms to make the place habitable. Jenna and Trevor were to sleep there with their children and the rest of us set about erecting our tents on the river bank. By now, the beer and wine was flowing and humour was at a high.

We had been having an idyllic time, fishing, boating, eating, drinking, talking, and just enjoying the wonderful ambience of the African bush - as one does on the banks of that incredible river. On the 2nd January we had spent the morning fishing, drifted down the river for a late afternoon drink, returned to camp, had a wonderful, gourmet-type meal - in true Zimbabwe fashion we had taken two cooks with us, who even managed to produce freshly baked bread each day.

We had been sitting around reminiscing about the *good, old, bad days*, enjoying the odd glass of wine or six as one often does, listening to the *noises of the night* – the loud barks of the baboons, the hoarse coughs of the hyenas, the occasional roar of lions and the musical sound of the Christmas beetles. Just beautiful!

At about 9:30pm we all decided to retire for the night. Isn't it amazing how tired one gets doing nothing all day? I settled into my little tent (one of those two-man affairs made for undersized midgets!). It was extremely hot and sultry, so after about an hour of tossing and turning I decided to sleep on the stretcher I had outside my tent. The tent was too small for the stretcher to fit inside! I must admit, that as I arranged my pillow and sheet on the stretcher, the thought of wild animals did cross my mind but I instantly dismissed the idea, settled down and was soon fast asleep.

At ten to midnight I was jerked to wakefulness by the sound of the scrunching of bones and the most disgusting smell. Confused and disorientated, at first I didn't know what was going on, but I soon realised that the bones being scrunched were my bones, as a hyena bit into my face and hand and started dragging me up the steep slope. I screamed and screamed, fighting desperately as though my life depended on it – which I suppose it really did – and thinking that my end was insight! It must have been only a few seconds before the brute, realising that he'd bitten off more than he could chew, let me go and vanished into the night. As I knelt in the dirt, the blood pouring from my face, I realised that my hands and feet still worked and that I could still think so I must be all right!

I was actually a bit of a mess. My eye was in my ear, my ear was hanging off, my face was a bloody pulp, my thumb was nearly detached from my hand and my arms were torn to shreds.

My son-in-law, Trevor Gilbert and a friend picked me up and carried me to the thatched A-frame, where they sat me in the light. My daughter Jenna and her friend, Kim, then proceeded to put me together, cleaning up all my wounds and bandaging them. What a dreadful thing for a daughter to have to do for her mother, but both she and Kim managed superbly. Luckily, Trevor is one of those people who have to have the best of everything and so his First Aid Kit was the best on the market. It included saline drips which were used to clean all my wounds.

I was put onto the front passenger seat of the 4x4 that had been laid flat. Geoff held my head and Trevor drove me back through the bush to the hospital in Kariba, the nearest small town. I could hear Trevor and Geoff talking.

"Don't let her fall asleep Geoff," said Trevor. "She's lost lots of blood, she'll go into shock."

Every elephant and his friend seemed to be on that bush track that night and weren't too keen to get out of the way.

"Oh no!" yelled Trevor, "The elies are blocking the way. I can't get through."

"Just keep driving," said the ever-stoic Geoff. Trevor did and miraculously the elephants parted and let us through.

Eventually we arrived at Kariba at 2:30am and met the only piece of negativity we found when the duty nurses took one look at me and said, "Maiwee, maiwee! You cannot come here, we have no facilities. You must go to Harare."

Harare was another five hours drive away.

Luckily, two Cuban doctors appeared and immediately put me on a drip, administered painkillers, gave me an anti-tetanus injection, rabies vaccine and sewed up my thumb, apologising that they could do nothing for my face. They really gave me a good Z$120 worth which was what government clinics charged at that time.

In the meantime, after many phone calls, Trevor had managed to get hold of my sister, Barbara, in Harare. She contacted MARS, the Medical Air Rescue Service who agreed to come and fetch me. BUT, can you believe this? As there was an air-traffic controllers' strike in progress they were only able to land in Kariba when it was light.

Trevor, meanwhile, went into Kariba town to find the airport manager who had the keys to open up the airport. After much running around he came back with the manager's keys, just for the main security gate! Just before the expected time of the plane's arrival, Trevor was going to transfer me into his car so that there would be no delay at the airport when the plane landed. Here, the hospital staff refused to release me as they were 'responsible' for me and I had to travel in the hospital ambulance, but the driver would have to 'jump start' it for them after they had located him! Well, Trevor took one look at the ambulance and said that under no circumstances was his mother-in-law going in that 'death trap'! It really was horrendous, literally tied together with wire and tyres worn down to the metal! After much argument, Trevor drove to the airport to fetch the doctor and nursing sister to bring them back to Kariba Hospital.

They were great, examined me and agreed that I could travel in Trevor's 4x4 with them in attendance. Reaching the airport, the pilots apologised for not arriving sooner. I was soon ensconced in the Air Ambulance and in the air. The MARS doctor and sister were superb, very efficient and reassuring. During the flight they radioed ahead to the Avenues Clinic for a receiving surgeon to be waiting for me and to have a plastic surgeon on stand-by.

Upon my arrival at the Clinic, things went pretty much according to the TV Soaps, where I was handed over to the doctors and plastic surgeon, X-rayed, prepared for theatre, operated on, and then sent to the wards. Contrary to what I had been led to believe would happen in Zimbabwe at that time, my treatment and nursing was second to none and I have nothing but praise for all the people who attended to me. They were all highly skilled and very caring. We were so fortunate in that country to have had so many dedicated and highly thought of specialists practising there – quite a few of whom are still doing so.

Meanwhile my poor husband, who was in Chipinge where we lived at that time, had been told by my elder daughter Alison, who lived on a farm in Middle Sabi, that I had been attacked and dragged by my head by a hyena, the message she had received. Fearing the worst, he packed his funeral suit and set off for Harare, planning my service and choosing hymns on the way. He was actually highly relieved to see me alive!

I am sure that I was on half the prayer lists in the country upon my arrival in Harare and probably most of the others by the time I was in theatre. It was incredible how quickly the news had spread. I do believe that I am living proof that prayers are answered. From the moment that hyena let go of me, everything was positive.

I did lose my eye but the surgeon managed to re-attach my eye-lid, which is a big plus for holding in a false eye. He had hopes of finding tear ducts but this was not to be. After the first operation he thought he would have to do a couple of skin grafts, but during the second operation ten days later he found that it wasn't necessary. My face, especially the eyelid, was very swollen, needing to be massaged for at least half an hour three times a day. This, my husband did. I would then lie back and revel in the joys of formication (note the letter "m"), following the stimulation to my face. I never cease to be amazed at my recovery. Having been for various neuro-scans, it appeared that the nerves in both my face and hands were working - more or less.

The bone man managed to put my very *graunched* hand back together with skewers and skill. It took him three operations and six months but I have just about full movement back. When I said to him,

'Thank you so much, I was really worried about my hand,' his reply was,

'So was I – but you know something? This had so much to do with getting it right.' – and he tapped me on the head!

Fourteen operations later, I am amazed at my recovery and cannot believe how good my face is when I look back and remember how mutilated it was. My eye socket was reconstructed, using the mucus membrane from my mouth, so that it could hold a glass eye which looks fine but doesn't see too well.

Much worse things happen to other people. I am still alive. My injuries could have been much more horrific. The response of my family and friends, and total strangers were wonderful. The prayers, support, good wishes, flowers and gifts given to us by so many were unbelievable. People raised and donated, what I considered to be, vast amounts of money to help towards my medical expenses. This I found very difficult to accept as I had always been one of the people who organised this sort of thing.

Zimbabwe was, and still is, still a very caring society to live in. People saw what needed doing and did it. I arrived home to a full freezer and fridge and a house full of flowers and meals. My little school was in perfect running order, as I knew it would be.

When something horrific happens to you, it makes you stop and take stock of all that you have. It enables you to put things into perspective and to realize what is important in your life. So often we take everything for granted and don't appreciate all that is good in our lives. We let little things niggle us, tend to be judgmental and let things get out of proportion. Pull yourself up short. Think about your life and all you have to be thankful for. Focus on what is important. Show your gratitude. Dare to survive.

Since my 'Hyena Incident' I have met a vast number of people who have survived incredible traumas and believe they have come out as better people. They have such positive attitudes and are wonderful people and an inspiration to speak to.

They dared to survive. You don't have to go through trauma to have a survival attitude and a positive mindset. Remember that life is ten percent what happens to you and ninety percent how you respond to it. You have the ability to respond and therefore the 'responsibility' for your life. Our past responses have brought us to the place where we are at now. Is it a place that you like to be in or does it need changing? You can change your life if you really want to. Live life positively. Dare to survive, thrive and lead a wonderful life.

CHAPTER TWO
DARE TO LAUGH

Humour is infectious. The sound of roaring laughter is far more contagious than any cough, sniffle, or sneeze. When laughter is shared, it binds people together and increases happiness and intimacy. In addition to the domino effect of joy and amusement, laughter also triggers healthy physical changes in the body. Humour and laughter strengthen your immune system, boost your energy, diminish pain, and protect you from the damaging effects of stress. Best of all, this priceless medicine is fun, free, and easy to use. Laughter is strong medicine for mind and body.

"Your sense of humour is one of the most powerful tools you have to make certain that your daily mood and emotional state support good health."~ Paul E. McGhee, Ph.D.

Laughter is a powerful antidote to stress, pain, and conflict. Nothing works faster or more dependably to bring your mind and body back into balance than a good laugh. Humour lightens your burdens, inspires hopes, connects you to others, and keeps you grounded, focused, and alert. With so much power to heal and renew, the ability to laugh easily and frequently is a tremendous resource for surmounting problems, enhancing your relationships, and supporting both physical and emotional health.

Laughter is good for your health. It relaxes the whole body. A good, hearty laugh relieves physical tension and stress, leaving your muscles relaxed for up to forty-five minutes afterwards. Laughter boosts the immune system. It decreases stress hormones and increases immune cells and infection-fighting antibodies, thus improving your resistance to disease. Laughter triggers the release of endorphins, the body's natural feel-good chemicals. Endorphins promote an overall sense of well-being and can even temporarily relieve pain. Laughter protects the heart, improving the function of blood vessels and increasing blood flow, which can help protect you against a heart attack and other cardiovascular problems.

With all those good results from just having a laugh you have to do it don't you?

Things never seem so bad when you can laugh at them and at yourself! Laughter is after all the enthusiasm of energy. To keep that mental energy going you really need to have humour and laughter in your life.

Even a few hours after being in hospital following the hyena attack my family; friends and I were in gales of laughter.

Losing an eye means your depth perception goes, so I was forever misjudging distances and dropping things all over the place. Kept bashing my head on things because I hadn't seen them. I just kept laughing and learning and found it amazing how quickly I learnt to judge distances and become aware of where things were on my blind side.

I also had a big problem with my 'knickers'. Do you know how difficult it is to 'hoik' your pants up and down when both your hands are heavily bandaged? I sent my delightful nephew, Michael out to buy me some BIG knickers, which I could just hook onto my thumbs to slip up and down. Mike did just as I asked and came back with really enormous bloomers, real 'granny' pants – no lace or glamour at all. Even wearing them was a laugh. Or what about w…. oh no, we'd better not go there. How about cleaning your teeth? Just about impossible to hold a tooth brush let alone scrub anything with it! These incidents certainly caused much hilarity.

As for smelling the coffee, you know how great it is when the aroma of fresh coffee comes wafting to you and your mouth begins to water in anticipation. Not so when your salivary gland has been punctured through your ear– all you get is an earful of saliva!

A few days after I had come out of hospital I had been sent to see Mr. Rivron, an 86 year old oculist, who had come out of retirement especially to help me out, as there were no other oculists left in Zimbabwe. He was a lovely old man who eventually found a brown eye – mine are blue – to pop into my much damaged eye socket. My sister and I thanked him profusely and then waited on the pavement outside for a lift. Well, that was a real insight into human behaviour – very interesting. I was not a very pretty sight but as Africans passed they put their faces right up to mine, staring at me for as long as they could. They would then say,

'Oh sorry Madam, so sorry!' or some such thing.

Europeans, on the other hand, had a quick glance and scurried by as fast as they could.

My sister and I really enjoyed ourselves deciding how people were going to react to my appearance and had a good laugh when they did react as we had grown to expect!

Kids are funny too.

Just after I'd had my artificial eye fitted I was sitting reading to my grandchildren when I realized that four year old Daniel was really staring at me.

'Can you really take your eye out Granny?' 'Yes.'

'Oh please take your eye out Granny; take your eye out, please.'

After much persuasion I did and then popped it in again.

'Take your other eye out Granny. Go on. Please take your other eye out.'

I didn't! But Daniel and the other grandkids enjoyed the humour of the situation and I think it helped them to cope with me looking so awful at the time.

One evening our whole family was gathered at my Mum's house and we were discussing sleeping arrangements. It was decided that I would share rooms with my Mum – everyone called her Mum.

Andrea, aged five, looked at her very seriously and said,

'Be very careful sleeping with my Granny. Her eye doesn't close and she'll stare at you all night long. That's a bit spooky!'

About five weeks after the attack, my temporary artificial eye fell out. PROBLEM. Medical supplies were very short in Zimbabwe at that time. We had to find a stent so that the damaged socket wouldn't shrink.

'Go round and see the ophthalmologist, at once', said my surgeon.' He has a stent for you.' Great!

Mr. Sparrow was a tall, gaunt, eccentric looking man with long, grey hair coiled in a French pleat and white powder on his cheeks. In rather flowing garments he appeared more like an artist than a medical man. He showed me into his room and indicated where I should sit by waving a rather holey, white damask table napkin under my nose before placing it on the seat of a chair!

I explained the situation to him.

"You mean you had a perfectly good, seeing eye there, this creature simply removed it and now you don't have an eye?'

"Yes."

"Amazing", he said. "Amazing." He proceeded to examine me and put drops in both eyes.

"What's that for?"

"Anesthetic to deaden any feeling." Oh my gosh, I wonder what he's going to do to me?

He took out his light and gazed intently into my good eye and then did the same to my 'empty' eye socket.

He then covered my left eye socket with a card. 'Read the letters on the chart on the wall.' I did.

He then covered the good eye. You know what I'm going to say don't you? 'Read the letters on the chart on the wall.'

'I can't read a thing. I can't see. I don't have an eye to see with on that side.

'Oh don't you? Amazing, amazing.'

Once again I explained why I was there, whereupon he leapt up and came back with a large bag of what looked like marbles, but were actually glass eyes.

He scrabbled through the marble bag picking up various ones and tried to see if they would fit in my empty socket, all very hygienic as you can imagine.

Eventually he looked up, gazed at my face for a long time.

'You know what you really need,' he said, 'What you really need is a stent!'

'Yes, I know. That's what I've come for.'

'Oh dear, well I haven't got any stents!'

I did actually wonder if my plastic surgeon had sent me to see Mr. Sparrow for a good laugh!

And, of course, that's not a bad thing, because laughter keeps you focused. As I said before, it's the energy of enthusiasm.

Even death has a funny side. The late Bill Goves, the father of professional speaking, told a wonderful story of a family taking their deceased father across country by plane. For the first time in his life, this guy was forced to have a first class ticket. Imagine that, travelling 'cattle class' all his life and then, when he's flying in a box, he gets to go first class – just at the time when he can't really enjoy the hot towels, the free champagne and all the other extras of flying first class.

That reminds me of a time when I was teaching at a Greek School. Two of the children, a brother and sister, were absent one day. The following day I asked them where they'd been.

'We went to the cemetery.'

'Oh, did you go to a funeral?'

'No, we went to dig up Grandpa.'

'Why did you do that?'

'Granny wants to take him back to Greece.'

Well, I couldn't help myself, I just burst out laughing with this vision in my mind of Granny, a typical Greek matriarch, all in black, as wide as she was tall, sitting next to Grandpa, a skeleton dressed in his best coat and hat, flying off to Greece, both sitting there all prim and proper. I felt really bad about my outburst and later tried to apologise to the children's mother, as the children had told her about my laughter. The more I tried to explain and apologise, the worst it got. She ended up by saying,

'We all have to do what we have to do!'

And yes we do.

So laugh. It is so good for you. No matter what you are hit with, it's essential to engage your *Mindset Energy* to keep your positive attitude on the upswing with a great sense of humour. A laugh really does so much for you – mind, body and soul! Dare to laugh. Go on.

CHAPTER THREE
DARE TO FALL IN LOVE

Think about love. We love all sorts of things. We love our family, our friends, our home, our school, our job, the book we're reading. The list goes on and on. You love something and then one day it's suddenly gone, or changed, or lost forever. But, somehow that doesn't stop your love. Maybe that's how you know it's the real thing. When love doesn't come with conditions and 'get out' clauses, when it doesn't have a 'best by' date, when you just give your love and never stop giving it and know that you never will – that's when it is real. That's when no-one can ever touch it or spoil it or take it away from you.

Do you have the mental energy to love totally and unconditionally? It takes guts and real positive mindset. I think that the easiest unconditional love is the love children initially have for their parents - and the love their parents give them is also usually unconditional.

As time goes by this can change, as both child and parent are being influenced by each other and by outside conditions. Are you strong enough to withstand those outside influences and not let what happens around you make any difference to your love? In a family relationship ties are usually strong and for the most part relationships are all encompassing and unconditional.

It is later, as we fall in love with others that it is often difficult to give ourselves in this way and it is even more difficult not to be affected by outside influences. Then we can see if it really is the 'real thing'.

I can clearly remember the first time I fell in love. I was five or six years old. I'd been chosen to be the Queen of the Fairies in our school play. I was in love with the leading man. I can even remember his name – David Dyke! And I knew he was in love with me because he just ignored me totally, all the time.

There I was lovely white tutu, sparkly crown in my blonde curls, shining wand and wings and best of all – lipstick – wow bright red lipstick at five years old. I was loving it. I had to run across the stage saying 'Now I will call my maidens all.' Beckon them and run back across stage. Big voice, big gestures.

Off I went. 'Now I will call my maidens all.' Ran across the stage. Beckoned madly, turned, and tripped over my own feet, fell flat on my face. Tears, howls, bloody nose – blood everywhere, down my front, all over my beautiful tutu. Tears and more tears. What a disaster and what a way to end my first public performance!

But it didn't end there. The teacher picked me up, mopped me off and I carried on, very aware that the drops of blood on my tutu matched my bright red lipstick - and the King of the Fairies was still in love with me because he actually looked at me and spoke. He shrugged his shoulders and muttered one word, 'Girls!' I also think that that was probably the first time that engaging my mental energy and being positive about what happened to me really became a part of who I am.

I can't count the number of times 'I fell in love' during my teens, often it was 'being in love with being in love.' Only one, Tony, was my true love and we'll come back to him later.

Geoff was my hero. He came into my life when I was at College. In those days if you weren't married by the time you were twenty-two or three you were definitely on the shelf. He was five years older than me, tall and reddy-blonde and raced motor cycles fairly successfully. I thought he was wonderful. We became engaged on my twentieth birthday and were married sixteen months later.

We lived in a little thatched cottage with our sparse possessions. Some of our furniture was fashioned from wooden apple boxes covered in pieces of remnant material. When it rained we couldn't find a place in the bedroom where the water didn't drip through the roof onto our bed. We had fun together, enjoyed setting up our home and being a couple.

Two years later we set out on our adventure, travelling to America where Geoff hoped to continue his racing career. Unfortunately that didn't really materialize, although he did race a couple of times, but we did so many different things together. We took up deep-sea diving for a living, raced across the Navajo Desert and travelled as much as we could. Whilst in America, I fell pregnant with our elder daughter, Alison. We returned to Zimbabwe soon afterwards and set about designing and building our new home. Sixteen months after Alison's arrival, Jenna pitched up and our family was complete.

We were very happy and Geoff was very successful in his business. He owned and flew his own aeroplane and we led, what we considered to be, a great life. Unfortunately the 'War of Liberation' in Zimbabwe put a strain on our lives as Geoff was often on call-up and away – as were most young white men living there at that time. After fourteen years of marriage our relationship ended and I was devastated. This was when my Dad made me realize that I actually could make it on my own with my two beautiful daughters. Fortunately, Geoff and I remained good friends and had a close relationship even though we both remarried – and just before he died we both agreed that we still had a special love for each other, which was great.

The *grand passion* of my life began on my sixtieth birthday, although the real beginning was forty-three years before that.

His name is Tony. We met at a teen party whilst we were still at school. I was seventeen and he was eighteen. It was one of those "wow, heart racing, isn't he gorgeous" moments when he first asked me to dance. It was love at first sight for both of us. We spent the entire evening in each other's company, not believing how we both felt. We danced, held hands, snuck outside for a tentative kiss, cuddle, and just fell even deeper in love – as you do at that age.

Tony attended a boarding school in a town about three hundred kilometres away. Over the next few months, we were able to meet four more times. We went to the movies – with his father! Tony came and stayed at our house for a weekend and my dad lent us the car to go to a party at the local country club. We spent a couple of days at the Agricultural Show just wandering around hand in hand and having the occasional ride on the big wheel at Luna Park so that we could scream with excitement as we clung on to each other – as you do at that age!

Our last meeting was on 10th December 1963 at Salisbury railway station, in the then country of Rhodesia. Together with other friends and members of his family, we were gathered there to wish Tony bon voyage as he left to catch the ship in Cape Town for his trip to the UK to join the Royal Air Force as a navigator. I can remember going home feeling very flat at the idea of never seeing him again. I think I lay on my bed, listening to Cliff Richard's crooning voice and mooning over the loss of Tony for at least two days – as one did at that age.

My career path was also mapped out. I was to remain in Rhodesia to attend The Teacher College in Bulawayo for the next three years. I then had to work for the government for a further three years. Tony and I wrote to each other for a while but it petered out as things were very different in those days, post took ages, there were no emails, phoning was difficult and expensive, trips overseas were just out of the question at that time. It was far too difficult to keep in touch, with very little hope of being together.

Over the years we both qualified in our chosen fields, met other people, married in the same year. Tony had three sons, I had two daughters. We both thought of each other over the years and wondered what had become of the other. Tony started looking for me, and other friends he'd lost touch with, via the internet about eight years ago, but to no avail. Then, about four years ago, Tony put a 'seeking Diane Southon' (my maiden name) message on an ex-Rhodesian website, as a last resort. Quite a few people saw it and told me that a 'Tony' was looking for me. It took me about two days to compose an email to him, to which I received an immediate reply. It was great. We were instant friends and had so much to tell each other. Tony started phoning me and we would talk on the phone for hours. There was definite chemistry between us even then. We could not believe how we responded to each other.

By chance, I was actually going to Brisbane, where Tony had been living for the past thirty odd years, for my nephew's wedding. My sister and I arrived on my sixtieth birthday and there was Tony waiting at the airport. We saw each other for ten minutes then – and those same feelings that we had experienced on our first meeting all those years ago, reared up again. Tony and I were both married and our respective spouses knew there was a bond between us but 'allowed' us to meet in a public place. This we did, finding ourselves on Mt Coot-tha. We spent the whole two hours sitting opposite each other in the restaurant and talking nineteen to the dozen. We had a quick kiss and cuddle in the car park before Tony dropped me off. A few days later Tony phoned again and asked for another meeting – same place and same scenario. This time Tony asked me to marry him and I said yes even though we both knew this was an impossible dream. During the next four weeks of my holiday, as I toured Australia, Tony phoned daily, at least four or five times, and we decided that we had to be together no matter what.

We both had to tell our spouses and boy – naturally – the fireworks exploded or, as they say in the vernacular, 'the shit hit the fan!' We had a couple of months of "should we, shouldn't we?" before agreeing that we were definitely soul mates and needed to be together. I handed in my notice. I was the principal of a unique private school in a country town so a great scandal would have occurred if the locals knew that I was leaving my husband to run off with my very first boyfriend to go and live in Australia. They actually caught wind of it but very few people believed that such a respectable, up-standing head would behave in such a way!

I left Zimbabwe and met up with Tony in Johannesburg on 12th December 2006, forty-three years, just about to the day, after we had said goodbye on that railway station in Salisbury, Rhodesia. We spent a couple of months touring South Africa, just loving being together, living our dreams and fantasies, visiting Tony's mother and sisters, before going up to Zimbabwe so that Tony could meet my family and friends.

We returned to Brisbane where we set up home together. We felt we were just made for each other. We were like a couple of silly teenagers together. We laughed, romanced, listened to music, danced, walked, sang, loved, cooked, travelled, experienced everything we could and just thoroughly enjoyed being in each other's company. It was wonderful.

We took some fabulous trips. We set out on an outback safari up to Darwin, Broome and Alice Springs. That was a good relationship tester as we were camping for a good deal of the time and sometimes, in places like the roadside of the Tanami Desert, where there were no facilities at all. We really got to know one another well. We toured New South Wales and discovered how fond of wine we both were. We also had a good evening reminiscing about our long lost youth when we came upon an Elvis Evening whilst on our travels – just our era!

We took a trip back to Zimbabwe when my daughter became ill with cancer and subsequently died in 2007. Although very sad, it was great for Tony to see the wonderful community spirit that abounded there, given the dire political situation in that country. At the beginning of 2007, we had spent six weeks in New Zealand where we shared fantastic experiences such as climbing the Franz Joseph Glacier and swimming with dolphins. New Zealanders will tell you that the weather does not matter but it does! October saw us attending a conference in the Bahamas. Conference was great but the Bahamas is a bit over-rated in our opinion – and a long, long way away! We have done so much in the time we have been together.

Three years later, we are still together, still very much in love. We enjoy outings to the theatre and concerts. We have joined a gym where we go three times a week and enjoy kayaking along the various creeks and rivers around Brisbane. We enjoy walking and picnicking. We have had many challenges on the way, not least being great feelings of guilt over abandoning our respective partners. Because of these guilt feelings there were a few episodes of Tony returning to his previous life. However, we do know that we are made for each other. We are total soul mates and just revel in being together. We had a wonderful commitment ceremony in September 2008, when our friends and family joined us as we pledged ourselves to each other.

We have now started a business venture called Carter Health and Business Solutions where Tony is a management consultant and I complement him as a keynote speaker and workshop facilitator, following my passion of spreading the message of 'Attitude is All'. We also promote a great nutritional fruit juice called 'Monavie', because we know it is great and it also is a wonderful business opportunity for people. Tony and I work well together and we are a great team.

We love each other totally and unconditionally and to experience a grand passion such as this when one is in one's sixties is truly remarkable. I believe that very few people are fortunate enough to experience the depth of passion that Tony and I have for each other and we were truly blessed to have found each other at this stage in our lives. I will not tell you any more about our relationship, for as my daughter Jenna is always saying to me – "too much information Mom!"

Suffice to say, the best relationship is one in which your love for each other exceeds your need for each other. Great love and great achievements involve great risk. It has been said that the greatest risk in life is not to take a risk.

Sometimes you have to risk everything to find the only thing you need. The risk you do not take could be the one that could change your life forever, for the better.

Tony and I always approach love and cooking with reckless abandon – and it works for us. Go and follow your heart! Find your 'Grand Passion'! Dare to love.

CHAPTER FOUR
DARE TO PERCEIVE DIFFERENTLY

You know, perception clouds so much of what we think, feel and do. What would your perception be of a woman standing on a street corner singing –

'I want a man, I want a man'?

And what would your perception be of a woman standing on a street corner, tambourine in hand, singing –

'I want a man, I want a man, and I want a mansion in the sky'?

Yes, quite different I'm sure and yet their message and aims might be identical.

I have six really delightful grandchildren. Five-year-old Daniel said to me the other day,

'Granny, why is the skin on your arms so old?'

Well, Daniel has a far different perception of what old skin is than I do!

'Daniel, Granny's skin isn't old; it's just a bit wrinklier than yours. Aren't I your gorgeous Granny?'

All my grandchildren are programmed really well, so that when asked 'Who is gorgeous?' they all reply 'My Granny.'

'Yes you are my gorgeous Granny, but your skin is a bit old!'

You can't win!

It really is amazing how people look at things differently.

There was an Englishman and an Australian chatting in a bar and the Englishman said,

'Well old chap, I can't see myself ever going to Australia. Why, that's where they sent all the convicts.'

'That's funny mate,' replied the Australian, 'cos I can't see myself ever going to England. That's the place where all the convicts came from isn't it?'

Recently Tony and I were travelling across America. At every airport we stopped at in the States there were always people hurrying into the myriad of eating places that abounded in the airports and there they consumed vast amounts of food! On our first cross country flight we discovered why. The airline didn't feed you on board. Qantas feeds you, South African Airlines feeds you, British Airways feeds you and even Air Zimbabwe feeds you. BUT American Airlines doesn't feed you! It did offer you a few items that they had for sale but we discovered that these were extremely expensive and just about inedible. Now our perception of American Airlines is that it is the worst airline we have ever been on. Your perception may be different but this sure put us off American Airlines.

Also at the airports in America we found that everyone was walking straight towards us. We were keeping to our side of the walkway but these people didn't realize that they should be on the other side. After quite a time of bumping into people the penny dropped. Clink, clink! We were the ones on the wrong side! We were the folk that drove our cars on the left hand side of the road and automatically walked on the left hand side of the walkway. These Americans drove on the right hand side and automatically walked on the right hand side of the walkway. We were the ones out of kilter in their country! It's all a matter of perception!

I can remember as a little girl, growing up in England and going tobogganing down a steep mountain side on a tea tray. I had wonderful adventures at that time of my life. We went wading across a really deep lake, with the water lapping inside our huge wellies (gum boots), as we watched out for the alligators that were prolific in the lake. Not too many years later I discovered that the steep mountain side was actually a gently sloping railway embankment. The lake was a tiny farm pond, my huge wellies were all of six inches high and the alligators were actually tadpoles. It's all a matter of perception!

I was travelling on a train cross-country and in front of me sat a young mum with her about six-year-old son. She seemed to think that her boy needed shouting at and chastising on a regular basis, which she did in a really ugly voice. The poor guy couldn't do anything right and was really cheeky in answering her back. The mum's mobile phone rang and immediately her voice and demeanour changed as she chatted on the phone to her friend. You wouldn't have believed it was the same person. Amazingly for the whole time that his mum was on the phone – at least twenty minutes – the little boy changed and he was a happy, smiling, normal child. What a pity she doesn't appreciate him and speak to him as she does to her friends. Perception!

Recently my nephew's wife gave birth to their first child. We went to view the newest addition to the family clan.

'Come in. Come and see our boy. He's so perfect, he weighed 8.5 pounds at birth, his length was 53cm and the circumference of his head was… what was it again, Mike? Isn't he just perfect? Just look at his toes. They're long like mine but just curl at the ends like Mike's. Can you remember if Mike had such a mop of dark hair when he was born?' said Jules.

It just went on and on. They were both just so thrilled with their little son. Both were very hands on parents, handled little Samuel so lovingly and confidently that it was a joy to see them. They had tried long and hard to have him and I am sure that Sam will never be a pain to his parents just because their perception of him is so positive.

A while back, my former husband was putting up a fence along a field on our farm. Instructing one of the workers, he said,

'Run the poles along the boundary leaving a three metre gap between them, but when you get to the little stream, which is only one metre wide, put in two poles.'

Coming back a few hours later, Jim saw that the poles were in, three metres apart, but where the stream was, were two poles standing shoulder to shoulder on one side of the stream!

'I wanted you to put in two poles, one on either side of the stream.' 'You didn't tell me that Boss, you told me to put in two poles when I came to the stream!' All to do with perception!

These examples show how easy it is to make mistakes and take things the wrong way just because our perceptions of various things are different from those of other people. We also tend to be judgmental of other people, often those from a different background or culture, just because we have no perception of what their values or beliefs are. We often don't understand the reasoning behind some of their behaviour, and they probably don't understand the reasoning behind some of our behaviour. We need to be perceptive about this.

We need to dare to perceive things differently or at least with an open mind and more understanding, if we are to have a positive attitude when facing life. Dare to perceive differently - it will pay off.

CHAPTER FIVE
DARE TO GET YOUR PRIORITIES RIGHT

It was so bizarre. 'The potty, someone get the potty!'

There I was, trapped beneath my Dad, between the crashed motor-bike and concrete railings.

'The potty, will someone get the potty!'

That was my Mum's voice. What was she on about? Only seconds before she'd been yelling –

'Bob, Bob – watch out – you're going to crash.' Bob was my Dad.

We'd been coming back from a camping holiday, travelling in our motor-bike and sidecar and towing a camping trailer.

Suddenly, there'd been a cracking noise. We'd veered crazily across the road, gone into a sideways skid, slid right across the bridge and crashed into the concrete side of it. My Dad was thrown forward, crashing his head on the windscreen and then slumping hard onto the side of the bridge, totally knocked out.

I tied securely to him with our coat belts – we didn't wear crash-helmets in those days, but we were tied together for safety, can you believe it? - landed up beneath him. Sidecar and passengers were fine but the camping trailer turned onto its side and burst open.

Into the centre of the road – horror of horrors - rolled… the potty!

That's when my Mother yelled from inside the sidecar, 'Get the potty, oh dear, everyone can see it. Someone grab the potty and hide it!'

You'd think that no one else ever used one!

'Don't worry lady, I'll get it for you.' called a passerby who'd come to help.

Thankful that the errant potty was now out of sight, my Mum was then able to concentrate on her bloodied and 'knocked out' husband, I squashed beneath him, and her two younger children, frightened and crying.

She never lived that little incident down – the day hiding the potty took priority over her family!

Looking back on my life, I now realize that I often allowed myself to be '2nd Best' because I didn't have the mental toughness to go the extra mile and be the champion I could have been.

Remember - 'It's your attitude not your aptitude that determines your altitude.' To be the very best you can be, you have to be prepared to do what the ordinary or mediocre folk are not prepared to do.

I loved school and that's probably why I stayed in school, in one capacity or another, all my life. I joined in everything full-bore and you would most likely say that my school career was highly successful. I ended up as head girl, was in all the sports teams, debating team, lead roles in school plays, and passed all my exams – JUST! That's it, I would never exert myself, or put in the work and effort to do as well as I should have. I never achieved the results I could have. So, in that respect I was a failure because I let myself down so badly.

It was the same when I went to The Teachers' College. I was passionate about being a teacher but really not quite passionate enough. Again, I didn't go the extra mile and again I let myself down. I am a member of the 'baby boomers' – that big bulge of babies born after the Second World War. I think that we have turned out to be a pretty remarkable generation of people. My years at college were remarkable in that our 'year' was the first year that students ever attained triple distinctions. That's where I fell short. In my special field of English I was given a special assignment to read and review a book called 'Maria and the Red Barn'. It was the first 'melodrama' to be written. I didn't even know what a melodrama was in those days. I was so busy having a ball, chasing boys, no, letting the boys chase me, going out and I didn't read the book, I didn't even look up the word in the dictionary, I didn't write the assignment and I didn't get my third distinction because of it. I really let myself down. I wasn't the best I could have been. And this is something I have regretted all my life. I wasn't mentally tough. I didn't get my priorities right.

Don't you let yourself down? Get your priorities right. Be the best you can be at whatever you do and reach your full potential. The sky's the limit! You owe it to yourself. You are the one who must believe in yourself before others can. Prove that you are the best and strive to be the best. Dare to prioritise.

CHAPTER SIX
DARE TO LOOK BACK WITH NO REGRETS

Can you remember, as a child, skipping with a rope and chanting various inane little rhymes? 'Salt, mustard, vinegar, pepper' was one. Another that really confused me was, "I know a secret and I mustn't tell, I was born in a winkle shell." As a little girl, this really confounded me. If it's a secret why are you telling it? If you've told everyone, it's not a secret and besides which, you couldn't be born in a winkle shell – all too confusing. NOW, as a bigger girl, I am even more confused to discover I have been living a secret I didn't even know about.

I first had an inkling of the secret about thirty years ago when my first husband left me and our two children. My father said to me, 'So what's the problem? You are bright, beautiful and intelligent. You have a home, you have a career, and you have two wonderful daughters. You don't need him. You can cope on your own. You haven't got problems, you have a great life set out before you, with a couple of challenges in front of you. You have always managed to meet any challenges in your way. Go for it!' And that's just what I did. From then on I never had problems in my life, I only had challenges.

About two years ago, I had another inkling of the secret whilst staying with a friend in Bateman's Bay. She had to go out for the morning and left me with some DVDs to watch. They were Esther and Jerry Hicks' *Abraham*. I watched enthralled, thinking, 'This is me, this is how I live my life. Incredible!' When Heather returned home I just enthused about it all. Heather's reaction was one of amazement. 'Haven't you come across *The Secret*?' she asked. 'No,' I replied. 'But but this is all about *The Secret*,' she said.

Out came the book. I quickly devoured it from cover to cover. I knew this secret. I had been living it all my life without realising it. Have you discovered *The Secret*? Have you read the book or seen the DVD? It really is the most amazingly wise book I have ever read.

But what is *The Secret*? *The Secret* is the *Law of Attraction*. Everything that is coming into your life, you are attracting into your life. It's attracted to you by virtue of the images you are holding in your mind. It's what you are thinking. Whatever is going on in your mind, you are attracting to you. Thoughts become things. Through the power of thought, the law of attraction is always working, whether you believe it, understand it or not.

And this is why I know that I have been living my life by the secret without knowing I knew about it. I was just very fortunate in that, I am by nature, a positive person and therefore my thoughts tend to be positive ones. I have always looked on the glass as being half-full rather than half-empty. Everything is in the power of our mind and our thoughts.

Looking back over my life and analysing various events I can see clearly how the secret has been effective in my life. Even as a small child I just wanted to be happy, that was my mindset – and I was, I had a very happy childhood. Even then, I knew I wanted to be a teacher. I would line up my dolls, along with my younger sister and brother, and play 'school' for hours. I later became a teacher.

When it was that time in my life to marry, I dreamt of my 'Prince Charming' and discovered the man of my dreams – a blond Adonis who excitingly raced motorcycles all around the tracks of Africa. Like me, he wanted to travel and we set off on a year's adventure to America. Naturally, we produced two beautiful children. Our partnership eventually ended but over the years we remained very great friends which was something we both wanted

My second marriage wasn't so successful mainly, I think, because I wasn't putting out the right vibes to attract the type of man I wanted and needed. Over the years, I have had various teaching positions and have enjoyed them all, gaining a great deal of satisfaction from my teaching.

When I was attacked by a hyena, from the moment the animal let me go I knew I would be all right – and I was.

Five years ago, my daughter gave birth to a beautiful baby girl, Benedicte. She was born with a serious heart defect and flown to Johannesburg where she underwent open heart surgery at four days old. My daughter was extremely positive about the outcome, as we all were, and in spite of various difficulties during the operation, this little girl survived and today is a vibrant, happy, active child.

Over the last few years that I was a school principal in Zimbabwe I was often under threat. The country was in political turmoil and I was often warned that I was going to be arrested for such 'crimes' as putting up school fees to keep my school viable. I was harassed by trade union representatives and assaulted by the head of the Criminal Investigation Organisation. At that time, law and order had broken down and government officials basically did what they wanted to do. I knew that I could cope and win in these situations. These bullies were not going to get the better of me and they never did.

Nearly four years ago I made contact with the first love of my life, Tony. We had a dream of being together – and now we are.

Perhaps 2007 was not the best year of my life. The father of my children died suddenly of a heart attack just two weeks before our elder daughter died of pancreatic cancer. Then six weeks later my mother died. WOW! What a lot to contend with. Of course I mourned their passing but I looked for more. I had been so lucky to have them in my life. Although our marriage had broken up, Geoff had always been such a good friend to me, a solid sounding board and someone I could always depend on. My Mother was 86. She had led a full life. Everyone loved her. She missed my Father who had died 8 years previously and now she missed her eldest grand-daughter whom she had been so close to. I had been so fortunate in having such a loving, caring Mother and hoped that I had learnt a great deal from her. My daughter Alison's death was another matter but I was so lucky to have had such a wonderful, beautiful daughter for thirty-six years. She had made such an impact on so many people's lives. She left behind a caring husband who is now bringing up their three small children in an atmosphere of love that is Alison's legacy. Positive thinking makes life so much easier to cope with.

About a year ago Tony and I decided we needed to go into business. We discovered a home–based enterprise whose main product was personal development. Again that secret – the law of attraction was at work.

We did the course – awesome - and then in October went to a conference on self–development in the Bahamas. We nearly didn't go, for various reasons, but obviously we were meant to be there. We listened to two speakers who really inspired me. One especially, spoke about making life–changing decisions, setting your thoughts and changing your attitudes so that you can achieve anything you want.

By now, I was really aware of how the secret was working in my life and over the past year or so had been making positive efforts to help it work well for me. I had been playing with the idea of becoming a professional speaker for about two years but hadn't found a topic that I felt I was passionate enough to speak about with conviction. Now I had it. Those speakers had made me realise it. I wanted to help people turn their lives around by helping them to sort out their thoughts. I wanted to show them how the secret could work in their lives.

To do it, I had to become a better speaker than I was. And this is where this workshop came into my life. Back in Brisbane, after the conference, full of enthusiasm and inspiration, I went to find a course on the internet. This course leapt right out at me – that law of attraction working again!

So there I was, knowing that being there would change me into the great speaker I needed to be if I was to influence people to change their lives for the better. Expectation is a powerful attractive force.

We are at the place we are because of the way we have responded to what has come into our life. We are responsible for all that we have done. We have made the choices. The past is in the past. What happened then has gone. Learn from the past and move on with a positive attitude and mindset energy. Our future is in our hands and we need to know exactly what we want in our future. Plan it and do what is necessary to make it happen. Dare to look back with no regrets and go forward with enthusiasm knowing that you can achieve anything.

CHAPTER SEVEN
DARE TO ACHIEVE THE IMPOSSIBLE

We can do anything we want to, if we want to badly enough. The key words here are 'if we want to badly enough'. So often we half-heartedly say we want to do something but don't do anything about it. Things won't change if there is no action. We have to have the mindset energy to get our thoughts into motion so that we can fulfill our goals. If you don't get things into motion you don't really want to do it badly enough.

When I was about eight months pregnant with my first daughter I took my younger brother to a motocross meeting where he was competing. He was a good rider and I watched with pride and enthusiasm as he completed lap after lap of his races. Suddenly, things changed as a group of bikes hit the dirt right in front of me. Clive came off, slid across the track and was hit by another bike, then ridden over.

'I have to get to him!' I thought, running towards the four foot high fence that separated me from the track. I really had to be there beside him, so without thinking about it, I leapt over the fence and rushed to kneel in the dirt beside him.

'Go away, I'm fine. Where's my motorbike?' He jumped up, grabbed his motorbike and roared away, leaving me there, gazing after him as he roared away in a cloud of dust. I then had to find a way to get back to the other side of the fence. I couldn't jump it again as I now had no real reason for really wanting to do so. I eventually walked, for what seemed like miles, until I found a gate. But I really had proved that I could do anything if I really wanted to! No way would I normally be able to jump a fence that high.

This brings me back to being able to do or be anything you want to. The reason we often don't succeed with our dreams is because we don't really believe we can, and the reason we don't believe we can is because of our background, our beliefs – many of which are limiting factors. We are brought up with certain expectations of what is expected of us and so often we just accept our lot in life. But, we don't have to. We can move on and beyond, achieving the seemingly impossible – if we really want to.

It's like the dogs in the pen. Some fierce dogs were put into a run surrounded by an electric fence. They quickly learned to stay away from the fence after having received a shock or two. The electrical current was turned off, but those fierce dogs stayed docilely inside their run, not realising that they could move on and that the world was their oyster.

We need to be brave and bold in our dreams and our goal setting. Think outside the 'run', know that you can achieve anything – you just have to want it badly enough. With a positive mindset and the energy that goes with it you can set in motion all that is needed to achieve anything you desire. So dare to achieve the impossible because nothing is impossible! Just remember that it is up to you to make it happen. Dream, set goals and dare to go for it! Champions succeed because they don't believe it when people tell them that dreams are impossible. They are possible. Don't limit your beliefs. Dare to achieve the impossible because you can!

CHAPTER EIGHT

DARE TO FOLLOW YOUR DREAMS

Have you engaged your Mindset Energy lately? Haven't a clue what I'm talking about? Let me tell you a little story.

You may think that unemployment here in Australia is high at below 6% but you must see what it's like in Zimbabwe – 96%! It's a real problem for the people there.

'Oh Mischek things are so terrible, so terrible,' said Freddie. 'There is simply no work. My landlord, he is shouting – no money. My children are crying. They have no food and are hungry. My landlord is shouting, he has no rent from me. It is very terrible. We must find a jobbie!'

'Ah - But what can we do Freddie – there are simply no jobs around. You are right, it is very, very terrible.' Replied Mischek.

'Ah shamwari (friend) I have a plan that simply came into my head. It is like a dream. It is a very good dream. We will be very smart, very successful businessmen. We could fixie the roads.'

'How can we fixie the roads Freddie? We have no machinery.'

Now the roads in Zimbabwe are terrible, really cracked, broken down and very pot-holed. In fact, the pot-holes are so bad that the police there arrest you if you drive in a straight line - because they reckon you must be too drunk to swerve and miss the holes!

Freddie carried on. 'Ah but no Mischek, we don't need machinery, we just need some brickies and a hammer. It will be a very smart business. It is a very goodie plan.'

'Ah shamwari yes, I would like to be a smart businessman - But who will pay us?' asked Mischek.

'Everyone. The marungus (Europeans), the black chefs – they are all maninge (very) sad for their smart cars to get so buggered on these roads.'

So these two enterprising fellows collected rubble in a barrow, put up a sign – 'Volunteer workers – pliz donate us' - and set about filling in the potholes and they were quite right. The people in their smart cars were only too pleased to pay them for their 'volunteer work' and would throw them the odd million dollar note or two, which was probably worth about half a loaf of bread at that time. BUT, by the end of the day, Freddie and Mischek had made quite a good living. Wonderful.

Then, after a few days the novelty of actually having to work for a living began to wear off and Mischeck had another 'bright idea'.

'This working, it is hard, too hard Freddie. I now have a better plan that simply came into my head. This is an even better dream. What about we set up all our gear, and our very special sign in the mornings, then simply fill in one hole and just sit beside it for the rest of the day? That will be a much better business, much smarter, not so hard.'

'Mischek that is very good plan. Good idea. I think we should be smart businessmen. We are very clever road fixers now! Shake, shake - my shamwari, shake my hand.'

So that's what they did for that day– and the next – and the next. At first motorists continued to donate cash, but realized quite quickly that very little work was actually being done and stopped their donations. The two entrepreneurs moved on to another site and continued their 'fix one hole and sit all day plan'. It wasn't long before no more cash was forthcoming, as motorists realized that their goodwill was being exploited, and these two enterprising young men returned to the ranks of the unemployed and penniless!

'Oh Mischek my shamwari,' said Freddie, 'No pay now, we will have to make another plan for workie. Our business is not such a smart success. It was not such a good dream, it did not work. Maybe we should have kept with my first plan, which was the best dream. Now things are terrible again, very terrible!'

These two entrepreneurs certainly hadn't engaged their *Mindset Energy*. And now I think you know what I mean by *Mindset Energy*.

Here is another occasion when *Mindset Energy* is all important. Losing Weight! I know all the reasons why I should lose weight and I've got all the excuses why I don't. Let me tell you a little story.

I bumped into my South African friend Marie the other day.

'Ag, Diane, I've got a new diet for you – the *Don't count those calories Diet.*

Marie knows that I'm a walkover for any new diet.

'Great, tell me about it.'

'Well, you know when you open a packet of biscuits some are broken? Just eat the broken biscuits and you don't count those calories. Now, if you go out for lunch and eat less than the other person you don't count those calories either.'

'Marie - You must be joking! It can't work?'

'Ag, probably not, but I think I'll try it anyway, it sounds fun.'

'Oh Marie, I haven't lost any more weight for months. I've got to do something. I had to keep coming up for air when I was painting my toe nails yesterday.'

'Ag man, then you must be at the ideal weight for you if you've stayed there for so long.'

'Rubbish! I mean, does this spare tyre round my middle look 'ideal'? And, even worse - someone told me I looked obese the other day.'

'Obese. Ag no, 'plump' or 'well-rounded', yes, but not obese. I mean, obese, obese is such a - well, such an 'obese' word. It's revolting. All those globby, gluttonous, whitey, yellowy globules surrounding every organ in your body.'

'Yes and, inside all that is a thin person trying to get out. "Let me out, let me out, you're smothering me! I can't breathe. Help, help!" Just too awful. Do you know the feeling? But, I've still done some really suicidal things to the thin me inside. I've added to all the blubber it has to fight its way through.'

'Same here. I've even bought half a dozen donuts, saying that they were for the kids and then eaten them all myself on the way home!'

Well I have lost fifteen kilos. I feel better, look better and am so much fitter. Funny, when I first lost the fifteen kilograms I felt really slim. Now that I've been at this weight for quite a few months I feel fat again. I just have to lose the next twelve kilos. I will do it. I know I will. I owe it to myself. I've set my mind to it. I can visualize the new, slim me - active and healthy - gorgeous. I will get there.

And so can you if you just set your mind to it. You just need to be determined and persistent. Have a positive attitude. Stick with a weight loss program. You can be and do anything you want, - if you want it badly enough. Let the thin person that's inside you, out. Be slim, fit and healthy. You can do it! Remember that if you only 'sort of' follow a diet you will only 'sort of' lose weight!

If you set your goals and have a purpose, if you pursue those goals with passion and persistence, you will achieve them.

Engage your *Mindset Energy*. Focus on your goals. Make them reality. If you don't have the drive to enthusiastically follow through your goals – you won't succeed. Come on, dare to make your dreams a reality. Have you got the guts to do it?

CHAPTER NINE
DARE TO PERSIST

Now, my old friend, Sandy, was a different kettle of fish. He also lived in Zimbabwe and had been having a tough time for quite a few years. He had lost most of his farm and had been left just a few acres where he kept a couple of cows.

He was really depressed at losing his farm. He came from real pioneer farming stock. His father had carved a farm from virgin bush and Sandy had followed in his footsteps and had carved his farm from the virgin bush. Sandy hadn't worn a pair of shoes until he was sent to boarding school at the age of seven, and he'd never played with white children. His friends had all been black and he spoke their language like a native. To lose his farm, like so many others had done, was to lose his life. He couldn't believe that the people he had grown up with and helped all his life would do this to him.

He hung around the house generally feeling very morose and getting in his wife Wendy's way.

'For goodness sake, Sandy, go and find something to do!'

'What can I do, Wendy? I don't have a farm to run anymore.'

'Well go and find a way to make cheese, Sandy. I can't get se anywhere for neither love nor money. There's no cheese in any of the shops. No one has any.'

Well surprisingly, Sandy took up the challenge. He had a wonderful time finding recipes, experimenting and producing all kinds of delicious cheeses – and selling them. He had a really good product and had a waiting list of customers. He just couldn't keep up with demand. He was a different person, enjoying the challenge of using the milk from his few cows to produce all these wonderful, exotic cheeses. He was up and going and viable when he was evicted from his little bit of remaining land and had to relocate to the suburbs of the capital city Harare. Cheese was no longer a viable proposition, but never daunted, he went straight into a new venture.

As they left the farm, he had put many of the plants and palms from Wendy's plant nursery onto the back of a truck. He now runs a nursery of exotic plants and palms, using these plants as his root stock, from his two acre garden in Harare and is selling to all the embassies and political bigwigs. He is making a good living and is no longer in his wife's hair.

During this time, Sandy had a stroke which left him with difficulties in using his right arm and speech difficulties. He persevered to overcome these challenges then Sandy and his son-in-law were involved in an horrific car smash. Sandy's injuries were so bad that he couldn't be flown to Johannesburg for treatment as Jason was. Sandy spent weeks in hospital and had to have nurses caring for him, day and night, on his return home. Again, Sandy was determined to get better and back to his normal active self – and he did!

All his life, Sandy has persisted at whatever he wanted to do until he had achieved it. It wasn't always easy for him but even in adversity he was persistent, set goals and achieved them. Dare to persist so that you too can realize your dreams and reach your goals.

We were travelling along the road at a steady speed, on our way to a school boy rugby festival. Jill, a friend was sitting beside me and three of the team were in the back. Now the road was wide tar but, as we approached the small African towns and villages, the sides of the road would become very congested with women selling tomatoes and baskets, small children, chickens, goats, donkeys and the odd pigs.

'Watch out! Donkey!' Jill yelled. And sure enough, coming straight across our path of travel, was a very determined donkey, going at a very determined pace. I slammed on the anchors, closed my eyes and prayed - and screeched to a stop. It was all I could do. Had I swerved, I would have hit the people at the side of the road. As it was, I slammed into the donkey!

As we came to a halt, the donkey sprawled across the bonnet of my car, he glared at me through the shattered windshield, slid down the crumpled bonnet and stood and shook himself, braying loudly. 'Hee – haw. Hee-haw.' He then took off across the road at a brisk trot.Well, we all got out of the car to look at the damage. The boys pointed out all the broken and smashed bits to me but I was a bit worried about the boys when they stood in a huddle and giggled. 'Shock!' I thought.

Jill turned to me. 'Di,' she said,' You won't believe this!' and she pointed a few hundred metres down the road.There was our donkey. He had mounted a female donkey and was having the time of his life. You know what I mean? No wonder the boys were giggling!

That donkey really had *Mindset Energy*. He had a purpose, he pursued that purpose with passion and he was persistent. He wasn't going to let anything stand in his way – not even my car! Really, he should have been dead, or at least badly injured but instead he had made his dreams come true! You can too if you dare to persist!

CHAPTER TEN
DARE TO COPE WITH DEATH

Grief is like the waves of the ocean that roll out, leaving a sense of calm, and then rush back in to knock you off your feet.

Children are so adept at coping with death. They seem to have an acceptance of it which enables them to deal with it so well. My children had myriads of animals whilst they were growing up and as happens, quite a few of them met a sad end. This led to many happy hours, arranging special funerals, fashioning shrouds and coffins, carving headstones and preparing services and digging holes.

At one stage we had very special long-haired guinea pigs that had their own hair brushes, curlers, ribbons and clips. We were going away on a three month trip so we decided to board the guinea pigs out with our neighbours, the Durrans, who had three little girls who were dying to look after these very special little creatures.

The guinea pigs were taken to their holiday home with all the 'special instructions' that my two girls thought were necessary and off we went for our camping trip. On our return, our first stop was to the Durrans to see the guinea pigs. There they were, looking great and - big surprise - they had produced six babies whilst we were away. All the little girls were thrilled and there was much negotiation as to who should have which guinea pigs. We arranged to pick 'ours' up the following morning.

Well, the following morning arrived and I had a very distraught phone call from Jo Durran saying that, during the night, a dog had broken into the guinea pig cage, had killed all of them and eaten most of them! How was I to tell my children? I just did it. They shed a couple of tears and then Alison said,

'Well at least they had a nice holiday at the Durrans before they went to heaven.'

A little while later, the girls were given a baby chick who they called 'Henny Penny'. Are you surprised at the name? Well as Henny Penny matured he/she developed into Cocky Locky, though still called Penny. For some unknown reason Penny developed a great dislike for my Mother and would attack her every time she came to visit, which was quite often as she lived next door.

Eventually, Geoff and I decided that Penny had to be dispatched so we arranged that the gardener would do the deed early the next morning before the children were awake. Well, early next morning, we were woken up by the children rushing into our room shouting,

'Penny is dead, Penny is dead!'

Then, they rushed out again and then kept coming back in to give us periodic updates on the state of the disemboweling and plucking and all the other processes necessary to get a chicken ready for the pot. Later I asked them if they were sad about what had happened to Penny.

'Oh, a little bit, but he shouldn't have been so horrible to Mum.' Total acceptance!

When someone close to us dies our initial feelings of grief are deep and wrenching. Although the emotion of grief feels bad it is an emotion that we need to feel. It is not a negative emotion when used properly. Grief is a cleansing process that we need to go through when we lose someone dear to us. Grief is only a negative emotion when you stay in it longer than is necessary and it loses its therapeutic qualities. People who choose to grieve too long, use it as an excuse not to move forward, they choose to experience the negative side of grief.

Life is a series of experiences, each one of which makes us bigger and helps to build our character. The setbacks and grief that we endure help us in our onward journey. Acceptance of death as part of the deal of living is one of the things that can enrich our lives and assist us in living well.

The year 2007 was not the best year of my life. At the beginning of August my elder daughter Alison phoned me to say she was not feeling very well and would be going to Harare, five hundred kilometres away, to see the doctor. She and her husband Chris and their three small children drove up on the Monday. She saw the doctor on the Tuesday, a specialist on the Wednesday, had a scan on Thursday, which showed that she had cancer of the pancreas and liver, and was due to have an exploratory operation on the Friday. I had long chats on the phone to her father, Geoff, who lived in South Africa. I was in Australia. I wanted to be in Zimbabwe at this time so that I could be with both my daughters and their families. They both asked me to wait before I went so that I could be there when Alison was having her 'treatment' and would really need me. Jenna and her husband and family were actually in Johannesburg at the time where her little boy was having his tonsils sorted out. Geoff said that he would go then and I would follow when needed.

Early on the Friday morning, Jenna, my younger daughter, phoned to tell me that Geoff had had a heart attack and had died. I couldn't believe it. Geoff had always been my rock and support. Although we were divorced, we had remained exceptional friends and were always there for each other. I knew then that I just had to be with my daughters. Jenna and Trevor went down to Durban to help Geoff's wife, Avril, with funeral arrangements. I made plans to travel to Zimbabwe as quickly as I could.

Alison had her op the day that Geoff had died though no one had told her about his death. I arrived in Harare and went straight to the hospital to see Alison. The surgeon had literally opened her up, looked and sewn her up again. Alison knew her prognosis was not good. Pancreatic cancer is very difficult to diagnose and once it is discovered, it is usually too late to do anything about it and the patient has perhaps up to six months to live. Alison was amazingly accepting of this, being very concerned about getting her five year old son's trunk ready for his start at boarding school the following January, and in finding someone else for Chris, her husband. They had three small children, Daniel aged five, Benedicte three and Marc just one.

As it turned out, Alison only had another two weeks to live. They were the most amazing two weeks. Friends lent them a house to stay in, people brought round meals, fruit, vegetables, eggs, and everything they could possibly need. Alison's friends arrived from all over the place, including other countries. They are an amazing group of girls, all friends from schooldays. Chris' brother and sister-in-law from Zambia arrived to help. A birthday party was arranged for Benedicte's third birthday. The children played happily on and around Alison's bed, though Alison was often up and about as much as she was able. She even made a visit to the hairdresser a couple of days before she died.

Benedicte was due to go to Johannesburg for a checkup as she had been born with a defective heart and had had open heart surgery at four days old. Chris decided to take Alison to Jo'burg, too, for a second opinion. Early on the morning of the day they were due to go, I went to the house to help Alison get ready for the trip. She seemed very tired and a bit disorientated. Chris was out getting airline tickets and cash so I phoned the doctor who asked me to take Alison to see her as she couldn't leave her surgery.

Off we went. Alison was dehydrated and was put on a drip. She seemed to get better but then was not very aware of what was going on. She wasn't well enough to travel on a commercial airline and the Medical Air Rescue Service wasn't prepared to fly her out so it was decided that we would take her home. Unfortunately, we didn't have time to do that, as Alison quietly died at the doctor's rooms having given everyone who entered her room the most wonderful smile.

I am so thankful that she didn't suffer for very long. The time we had with her was very short but it was special. Alison still looked very beautiful when she died, her hair curled around her head and a wonderful expression of peace on her face.

I am always so thankful that I was so privileged to be her Mother.

Alison was a true 'free-spirit' and lived life fully. She was very independent and accomplished so much. She was liked by so many, the number of her friends is phenomenal. A great wife and mother, she adored her husband and children, cared for them deeply and was fiercely loyal. She was so brave too, as shown when held at gunpoint, by three armed intruders, for three hours in her home. She was eight months pregnant and carrying her two small children, one on each hip, whilst her husband was helpless as he'd been tied up with a sack over his head and threatened that if he moved his wife and children would be killed. She maintained her calm and protected her off-spring.

To have had her for thirty-six years was wonderful for me. To watch her grow and develop over the years was a marvel that I'm sure every mother appreciates. Often, I didn't understand her and I sometimes didn't read her right but she grew into the most beautiful and competent young woman. I was so proud of her and continue to be, just as I am of her sister who never ceases to astound me with her great capacity for coping with whatever she is confronted with.

Both my daughters have met the many 'challenges' in their lives with great fortitude and courage. They have been so supportive of the decisions I made in my life and have never been judgmental.

I don't 'do' sad anniversaries but I was so touched on the anniversaries of Alison's death by the number of her friends who contacted me to say how much they missed her and what a wonderful person she was.

As I sit here writing this, the tears are pouring down my face, but they are tears of joy and remembrance for a wonderful and precious daughter. Of course, I miss her and mourn her passing. There is never a day that goes by when I don't think of her. It is so sad that her children don't have her to love and hold them in life but I know that she is caring for them, loving them and looking out for them. She touched so many lives. She dared to live fully and she dared to cope with death and helped us to cope with her death, too.

Six weeks after Alison died, my Mother died too. She hadn't been very well, had to have an operation and then had a stroke. She died a few days later. She had missed my Father so much since his death eight years before. She had been very close to Alison and was devastated by her death. She found it a very difficult situation to deal with. She was well into her eighties and had led a full and happy life. Everyone loved her and she was a deeply caring person. I was privileged to have had her for a Mother, learnt so much from her and sincerely hope that I have inherited many of her good qualities.

At the time of her death, I felt great tranquillity for my Mother as I believed that she was in a better place now, a place where she wanted to be. When my Father had died ten years before, however, I had felt a tremendous loss as I relied on him so much because he was such a wise man, as well as a very caring and loving Father. He didn't really believe he was ready to leave us – but perhaps he was!

I find it so amazing that the people who are diagnosed with life threatening illnesses have so much bravery in them to cope with what they have to endure.

Sylvia, a friend from school and college days, was diagnosed with cancer quite a few years ago. She was great, kept positive through all the nasty treatments she had to undergo and afterwards, was said to be in remission. Unfortunately, at the beginning of the year, whilst visiting her family in Adelaide the cancer reared its ugly head again. The prognosis was awful. She had limited time left and her end would be painful. She couldn't fly back home to Zimbabwe.

'Fine', said Sylvia, 'Brian', her husband, 'will just have to come back here. We'll be able to enjoy the time I have left with our children and grand children.'

And that's just what she did. I phoned her regularly and she – and the doctors - were amazed that she was as good as she was, that she is still able to be as active as she was and going strong. Brian travelled back and forth from Zimbabwe to look after his farm there, and he always expected his wife to still be around on his return to Adelaide. This went on for many more months than anticipated until Sylvia unfortunately died in June 2009 after a very brave fight to live. She dared to live longer than anyone thought she would and although she accepted her illness she made sure she got everything she could out of the time she spent with her precious family. She dared to cope with death and so did her family.

Death is a difficult part of life for us to cope with but it is a definite certainty.

'The death of someone we know always reminds us that we are still alive - perhaps for some purpose which we ought to re-examine'. ~ Mignon McLaughlin, *The Neurotic's Notebook.*

'Death smiles at us all; all a man can do is smile back.' ~ From the movie *Gladiator.*

So, dare to cope with death so that you can live life to the full!

CHAPTER ELEVEN
DARE TO MAKE THE BEST OF EVERYTHING

What is so wonderful about our lives is the fact that we are responsible for them. We make our life what it is and the main way we do that is by making choices. One of the greatest choices is to always make the best of any situation we find ourselves in. Sometimes, others help us make the best of the situation that we're in.

Whilst Principal of Mvurachena School, I used to go out riding with some of the children after school had finished for the day. I was a fairly competent rider, the only thing I found difficult was hauling me up on to the poor animals back, so I had had a special wooden mounting block made which solved the problem.

So there we were, me and about half a dozen children, enjoying a canter along a track between a stand of gum trees and a field of maize (corn). Suddenly there was a rustle in the maize and my horse shied sharply away from the noise. She careered into one of the children's ponies which kicked out at her. She shied again, this time in the opposite direction, totally unseating me so that I flew through the air and landed in the dirt whilst my horse cantered off.

Luckily for me JP came to the rescue. JP was the only boy in the seventh grade class, along with twelve girls, who he coped with very well. He had a few learning problems but was a wiz at mental math's and was so practical. I called him my Item – 'it takes a man' – because he was able to deal with and fix any situation that came along. And that is just what JP did then. He sent one of the other boys off to catch my horse and, knowing that there was no way that I could get back on my horse by myself, when it was caught, he set about organising a make shift mounting block for me. He put the smaller children in charge of holding the horses, whilst the others collected sawn off gum poles lying around and piled them up so that I could stand on them to mount which I was able to do. I had had visions of myself walking back to school, so I was really glad that JP had taken over, sorted everything out and made the best of a difficult situation.

Here is another story where the best was made of the situation. It's 1969 and I'm in Tijuana, Mexico. It's fiesta time and the atmosphere is electric. People, dust, noise, laughter, heat, music, tequila and dancing. We'd spent most of the day enjoying – if you can call it that – the bull-fights and now our husbands were firmly ensconced in the long bar – as young husbands were wont to do! My friend Morag and I had decided to go for a walk and had been wandering the streets, chatting, window shopping, flirting with a group of guys across the street who had been wolf-whistling at us as only the Mexican and Spanish can do.

Suddenly this police car came roaring around the corner, lights flashing, sirens blaring 'beebah beebah beebah beebah', and screeched to a halt beside us. Within seconds, three policemen had surrounded us, guns pointing, shouting and screaming.

'Vite, vite. Hands in ze air.' 'Vite, vite. Hands in ze air.Hands in ze air!'

We were petrified. As neither of us spoke Spanish, we hadn't a clue what was going on. By now a crowd had gathered around us as we stood there, hands in the air and the guns still pointing at us. We were so embarrassed, as well as being really scared. One of the flirty guys from across the street came over and started talking to the police. There was lots of gesticulating and pointing at our legs.

The talking died down and our friend started to explain to us.

'Senorinas, problem. You have to have a license. You soliciting.

Shorts no allowed in this street. Better you go with the police. Big problem.'

Can you believe this? They thought we were prostitutes.

'We're not prossies, we're married, and we're respectable!'

'Better you go with the police. Big problem.' Gosh, what a situation to be in. We were bundled into the car, whilst the young man agreed to go and find our husbands in the long bar. Off we went, to the police station, sirens blowing and lights flashing. Beebah beebah.

Once there we were locked in adjoining cells. Boy were we scared.

'Are you okay Morag?' I called.

"No speak, no speak," yelled a very threatening policeman, waving his gun.

"Okay, no speak." We were in despair.

After what seemed like an eternity, but was only probably about half an hour, we heard Geoff and Earl's voices, from another room. Luckily Earl spoke fluent Spanish. We could hear a heated debate going on. What on earth was happening? Suddenly there was laughter and the whole tone changed.

Our threatening policeman returned this time brandishing a key. He let us out of the cells and smiling, ushered us into a room at the front of the police station. There we fell into the arms of our respective husbands, both of us crying with relief. Morag and I had to sign some papers. There was handshaking, laughter, slaps on backs and remarks passed between the policemen and our husbands.

Once outside, the men just fell about laughing – they had been in the Long Bar a long time! Morag and I were really indignant.

'We were really scared. Anything could have happened to us!'

'No problem girls. You are now fully paid up members of the Hookers Club. It was cheaper to buy you licences to solicit than to pay the hundred dollar fine!'

Our husbands sure had made the best of a bad situation! And I still have the licence to prove it!

I bet you never expected the writer of this book to be someone who had a prostitutes licence… long expired I might add.

Make the choice to always make the best of any situation you find yourself in. Make the choice to live your life to the ultimate and enjoy every minute of it - even if it's not quite what you expected. Dare to make the best of every situation, life can only get better for you.

CHAPTER TWELVE
DARE TO ENJOY RELATIONSHIPS

Relationships make life. Before we can have a good relationship with anyone else we really need to have a good relationship with ourselves. We need to know ourselves, connect with ourselves, and be comfortable with ourselves, like ourselves – in fact, love ourselves and, most important of all, be true to ourselves. If we aren't, how can we expect others to be?

I know that when I was in my teens, I had not really come to terms with who I was and what I looked like. I thought I was fat and unattractive. Looking at photos of myself from that time, I see that I wasn't bad at all. Now that I have gone through years of wear and tear, put on weight and am not so tight, taut and terrific, I am perfectly at ease and accepting of my body, have grown quite used to it through the years and really quite like it.

So it is with my relationship with myself, I have grown to love and accept who I am, imperfections and all. It is no good beating yourself up about mistakes made in the past, it is better to learn from them.

I know that there are some things that I have said and done in my past that I am ashamed of but I have learnt from them and moved on.

Relationships have a tremendous impact on all aspects of our lives, family, and work, social and spiritual. It is the people with whom we have relationships who colour and influence what we do and who we are. This is why it is so important that we build relationships with like-minded people, people who have similar aspirations to the ones that we have.

We need to set ourselves up to succeed in life and realise all our dreams and goals, making sure that our friends and the environment we move in are conducive to being able to attain all we desire. We are known by the company we keep. Is it the right company?

Do we really appreciate our family and our friends? Are we pleasant and considerate when we are with them? Do we let them know how we feel about them?

Just before I left Zimbabwe for Australia I wrote both my daughters long letters telling them how much I loved them, how proud I was of all their achievements and how I admired them for being the beautiful, caring and considerate young women wives and mothers they had matured into. Thank goodness I had because Alison, my elder daughter, died eight months later. I am so glad that I had taken the time to express my love for them and how much I appreciated them being such a special part of my life.

I did the same for my sister on her sixtieth birthday. My sister, Barbara, and I are very different, yet have a special affiliation and closeness which is very special. The way she cared for me after my hyena attack was exceptional and she and her partner, Robbie, could not have done enough for me. I am so pleased that I made the opportunity to let her know what she meant to me. Unfortunately, I didn't actually write down the feelings I had for my very special Mother, which I regret, but I did tell her a couple of years before and I am sure she remembered and knew just what a great and positive influence she had had on my life.

So often we take the people closest to us for granted and don't appreciate them enough. A few times I have told Tony how much I like certain things he does for me.

"Tony, that was really great of you to clean my shoes for me. Thank you."

I then asked him if there was anything that I had done that he especially liked. I told him it was a sort of game I was playing. He wasn't happy to 'play' at first but soon got into it and it is remarkable how many things we do or say that the other person really likes. Try it. It is a way of showing gratitude.

The great story-teller and speaker, Andy Andrews, tells this wonderful

story –

For fourteen years, we had a Dalmatian named Lucy. She was our 'dog-daughter' until we had 'real' children! Lucy was a part of the family and she was especially important to my wife. For years I watched how Polly treated her, and occasionally, it irritated me. I told her one day 'You know, sometimes I think you treat that dog better than you treat me.' (She agreed.) But I couldn't help noticing how Lucy behaved when Polly was around.

When Polly came into the house after a morning out, I'd often be on the phone. Maybe I would've said, 'Hi,' or if it was an important call, I might even have rendered a 'Shh.' If I was writing, we'd often say hello from across the room. Lucy, on the other hand, reacted totally different when Polly entered the room. When Polly entered, Lucy would stand up and wag her tail, as if to say 'Hey, it's my mom! I love you!' She'd walk over to Polly and lick her face, 'Ooooh, ooh, kiss, kiss, and kiss.' (She even did this if Polly had just been in the room five minutes before!)

One day, it occurred to me that maybe if I treated my wife as good as the dog treated my wife... then maybe my wife would treat me as good as she treated the dog!

Do you treat people who come into your presence with love and care? Do you greet your spouse, significant other, friends or family the way a loving family pet might treat you? Watch their faces as they respond to your loving and joyful approach, how it lifts them up and brings a smile to their faces.

It is also important that we show appreciation to the people we work with as well – the other *team members*. Isn't it amazing how often people chastise others when they've made a mistake but forget to praise for a job well done. People know when they have screwed up and naturally feel bad about it. They don't need other people aggravating their bad feelings. Move on. People don't make mistakes on purpose.

Relationships need to be worked on and developed. They don't just happen. This is so, just as much in business relationships, as in family or social relationships. And remember to have fun and laughter whilst you are building up your relationships. Fun and laughter are great for developing a relaxed atmosphere that is easy to let ourselves go in and of course, it is the enthusiasm of energy which keeps us positive and on an upswing.

Mvurachena School in Chipinge, Zimbabwe, where I was principal, had the most wonderful atmosphere in the staff room. Whether it was break-time or lunch-time, you would always hear gales of laughter as the staff members relaxed, teased and had fun. Parents used to love popping in to see what was going on. And I think that it is very important to have fun in the workplace as this helps relationships between team members to develop.

At the same time, it is important to cultivate a happy, relaxed atmosphere in the home so that family members can be in an environment where they can be true to themselves, develop their own characters and bond with other family members.

Always remember to be honest and open in your relationships, be true to yourself. Be who you really are. Don't pretend. Dare to have great, meaningful relationships. They will help to shape your life.

CHAPTER THIRTEEN
DARE TO MATURE

No matter what age anyone is; it is never the right age. We always want to be older or younger. When we are toddling, we want to be 'a big boy or girl'. When we're children, in single figures, we want to be in our teens and then we want to be in our twenties. When we get older, we want to be younger. I just know that life gets better all the time, and I just have so many things I still want to do and learn, I've got to keep going for a great many more years. As you mature you look at things with different eyes. An incident that happened to me on my way to work one day, brought this home to me.

Well, there I was standing at the edge of the road, waiting to cross. There's this guy standing beside me, a sort of ferally looking man of about forty and he says,

'Scuse me Mam, but it's okay to cross now.'

'Oh, thank you very much,' I say.

'No problem, my Grandma always taught me to help elderly people!'

Well it nearly did my head in, I have never, ever considered myself to be elderly. Mature YES. Elderly, NO.

I have a little bit of a problem about age, mainly because I don't feel as old as I actually am. Eventually, my little grandson sorted it out for me. I was sitting reading to Daniel.

'Granny, how old are you really?'

'Oh Daniel, I'm so old I can't even remember.'

'Well, you know what you must do Granny,' – and he looks up at me with his big blue eyes, all earnest looking,' You know what you must do, you must look in your clothes 'cos there's a label there that tells you how old you are. Mine says five to six!'

Well I laughed. Then I started to think about it. My clothes say sixteen or eighteen. Well, what a hot chick that makes me! What is even better, is that not so long ago I was twenty to twenty-two. It's amazing how the years roll off when you lose a bit of weight.

Then I looked at the labels in Tony's clothes. Now Tony is edging towards his allotted 'three score years and ten' so it was great to discover that his labels read XL – roman numerals for ten and fifty. If the ten is in front of the fifty, you take it away, so that makes Tony a mature forty. Wow. Imagine a hot chick like me, sixteen or eighteen, being with a mature guy of forty. And how cool that a mature guy who's forty can still catch a hot chick of sixteen or eighteen. It's all a matter of how you look at it, isn't it?

Wrinkles are good, men show 70,000 different facial expressions using their muscles – women 200,000! A survey showed that people are drawn to people who use all of these facial expressions. If you've had surgery to 'smooth' away wrinkles your face can't express all that you feel and people aren't so drawn to you.

I was sent the following in one of those emails that 'do' the rounds and just thought it expressed so simply and clearly everything that I felt.

'I would never trade my amazing friends, my wonderful life, and my loving family for less grey hair or a flatter belly. As I've aged, I've become kinder to and less critical of myself. I've become my own friend. I don't chide myself for eating that extra biscuit or chocolate, or for not making my bed, or for buying that silly cement gecko that I didn't need, but that looks so avant-garde on my patio. I am entitled to a treat, to be messy, to be extravagant. I have seen too many dear friends leave this world too soon, before they understood the great freedom that comes with aging.

Whose business is it if I choose to read or play on the computer until four am and sleep until midday? I will dance with myself to those wonderful tunes of the sixties and seventies and if I, at the same time, wish to weep over a lost love, then I will.

I will walk on the beach in a swimsuit that is stretched over a bulging body and will dive into the waves with abandon if I choose to, despite the pitying glances from the jet-set. They too will grow old.

I know I am sometimes forgetful, but then again, some of life is just as well forgotten. I eventually remember the important things.

Sure, over the years my heart has been broken. How can your heart not break when you lose a loved one, or when a child suffers, or even when someone's beloved pet gets hit by a car? But broken hearts are what gives us strength, understanding and compassion. A heart never broken is pristine and sterile and will never know the joy of being imperfect.

I am so blessed to have lived long enough to have my hair turning grey and to have my youthful laughs be forever etched on my face. So many have never laughed and so many have died before their hair could turn silver.

As you get older, it is easier to be positive. You care less about what others think. I don't question myself anymore. I've even earned the right to be wrong.

I like being older. It has set me free. I like the person I have become. I am not going to live forever, but whilst I am still here, I will not waste time lamenting what could have been, or worrying about what will be. And I shall eat dessert every single day at every meal – if I feel like it!'

I love that, I can relate to all of it. So all you baby boomers, I hope you feel like me, that your life so far has been a wonderful journey but that there is still so much to be experienced. And for all of you who are on your journey to where I am, you have so much to look forward to. Set your goals, dream your dreams and pursue them with persistence. Make your choices the right choices and the positive ones. Always remember that you are responsible for your life because you have the ability to respond to whatever comes your way.

You have so much still to experience. Life is yours for the living. Make it the best life and the greatest adventure that you can. As you journey through life, enjoy and benefit from whatever comes your way. Dare to mature – it's great! Dare to live!

PART TWO
THEY DARED!

INTRODUCTION

Since the idea for writing this book entered my head, I have come across some amazing people, people who have 'Dared to Live'. They were confronted with daunting challenges, yet all have come to terms with the challenges and turned them into opportunities, not allowing the problems they faced to stand in the way of their lives. They engaged their '*Mindset Energy*'. They are beautiful and brave people from whom I have learnt so much. I feel so privileged that they have touched my life.

Julie Christie Scott is a young woman whom I have known for quite a long time in Zimbabwe. The last time I saw her was in hospital soon after her accident when she was in a really bad way. It has been wonderful to learn of Julie's grit and determination to return to good health and to put her life together again. An inspiring story.

When I first heard Steven Scharenguivel's story I was horrified that a child should have had to endure so much. It is a great testimony to Steven's inner strength, faith and positive attitude that he has developed into a winner- a warm, loving sincere person with great ambitions.

Simone Riddell is a young colleague of mine from a programmer on Women's Health that we both work in. She always came across as a very special young lady and one day let slip all that she had gone through when she discovered that she had cancer. She went through a grueling ordeal as she came to terms with this, but came out on top.

Stacey Huish is a successful, young business woman who told me all she went through with an abusive childhood, which led her to use drugs as a way to deal with her memories. Facing up to her challenge, she has turned her life around and is succeeding in all she does.

A special affinity arose between Tracy Eather and me because we had both lost daughters through cancer. Unfortunately, Tracy's daughter Amanda went through a great deal of pain and suffering with melanoma cancer. Tracy promised her daughter that her death would not be in vain and set up a foundation to carry out this promise.

I met Brian Huack through various business networking functions. Tall and good-looking Brian exudes charm and confidence, never letting his blindness in anyway infringe on what he wants to do. He aims high and goes for it!

Jaleesa Pon is the most appealing teenager I have ever met. It is amazing what I have learnt from her. She is full of *Mindset Energy* and I have included her story in this section of the book because she is such a shining example of someone who goes all out for what they want.

I thank, most sincerely, all these wonderful people for allowing me to share their stories and pass them on. They are an inspiration to us. I know that their lives will be blessed and they will continue to inspire us to greater endeavours. Thank you all for touching my life and so many other lives.

You are all survivors and thrivers. You dare to live.

JULIE DARED TO SURVIVE A CAR ACCIDENT

BY JULIE CHRISTIE SCOTT

My name is Julie Christie Scott and I live in Harare, Zimbabwe. Four years ago, when I was thirty-six years old and single, I had a serious car accident. What I went through tested my capabilities to the limit, and it changed my life forever. This is my story.

Wednesday the 8th December 2004 started like any other ordinary day. I was busy at work all day, and then went to have dinner with a girlfriend of mine, at a restaurant we both liked. We shared a bottle of wine, laughed and talked, and said our goodbyes before 10:00pm It started to drizzle as I set off home, but I was tired and eager to get back to my flat, and so I drove quickly in my little Mazda 323. As I turned on to a winding road a few kilometres from my destination, I was blinded by a pair of headlights coming towards me in the distance. I braked sharply but on the wet road, and with bad tyres, my car skidded violently. I saw myself heading towards a tree, at speed, and there was nothing I could do.

The next few hours were a blur. I was in and out of consciousness but I was trapped in the car – I had hit the tree with the right front of the car and with such an impact that the right front tyre pinned my inner left thigh to my seat (I later had photographs of the *tyre print* bruises on my leg – I should have been Pirelli calendar girl for December 2004!) and the steering wheel crushed my chest.

The lights of the car had gone out and it was raining, and the car that had dazzled me, plus several others which passed, did not see me on the side of the road. I was eventually found by some patrolling policemen four hours later. They called the fire brigade and I was cut out of my vehicle. I can remember parts of this very clearly, especially being put on to a stretcher board, and I could feel glass digging into the back of my head.

To cut a very long story short, I ended up in the casualty department of Avenues Clinic, Harare, where I was stabilized and underwent a series of X-rays. I couldn't move and at that stage I actually couldn't feel any pain. I think I was in shock and I was in and out of consciousness as well, and also now on morphine. I had broken many bones, and had cuts and bruises all over. There wasn't an orthopaedic surgeon available at first, and I had to wait until the following day before I was taken into theatre for them to try and patch me up. Operating began, but had to stop after a few hours – my lungs had filled with fluid and my blood pressure was dangerously low. I ended up on life support for the next forty-eight hours.

When I awoke, I was in intensive care, with plaster casts on various parts of my body, stitches in my chin, and numerous tubes coming out of my nose and chest. The only family I had there was a caring uncle and aunt who live in Harare – my parents had recently gone to the States to have Christmas with my sister and brother-in-law, as my sister was recently in remission from leukemia, and they were unable to get back as all flights to Africa were full over that period. It was also better for them to be near a telephone. My brother and his family lived in Australia, and my boyfriend was away caddying on the European Golf Tour. I am forever grateful to my wonderfully kind and caring friends and work colleagues, who gravitated to offer assistance. No one was sure what was going to happen to me as my injuries were too serious to tackle in Zimbabwe, so my international medical aid was contacted. At short notice, my brother left work and home and flew from Perth to be with me, and my boyfriend also returned as soon as he could.

It turned out that I had a compound fracture of my right ankle and several broken bones in my foot, a broken right tibia in the lower leg, broken right knee, broken radius and ulna of the right arm and a smashed right hand. My left leg had bad cuts and bruises and I had a broken left elbow and shattered left shoulder. I also had seven broken ribs, which were not found at first. Miraculously, my spine was intact although my pelvis was out of alignment, and I did not have internal or head injuries. My chin had split through to the jaw bone but this had been stitched, pretty well at that. Apart from that, I had some serious cuts which required stitching, and numerous bruises.

The pain was indescribable and I remember wondering where I hurt the most. I was on morphine but somehow I could still feel pain. I couldn't move and nurses had to lift me and also turn me over to prevent bed sores. This is not recommended with seven broken ribs – I am a quiet person by nature but even I could not refrain from screaming on those occasions! Because of the drugs I was on, and the fact that no one had actually given me a prognosis, I wasn't quite able to grasp the situation. I am not sure what I would have done, had I known what lay ahead. I did know that I was lucky to be alive, that my car was a write-off, and that my shoes had had to be prised out with a crowbar from beneath the brake and accelerator pedals. How I had managed to get out of there, I did not know.

I spent ten days flat on my back in hospital in Harare, Zimbabwe while I was stabilised and Interglobal, my international medical aid, sorted out the logistics for me to be flown to Johannesburg, South Africa. My brother and boyfriend were there, and friends visited daily. I was in touch with my parents and family in America every day. One night, we were told a plane was waiting and I was taken by ambulance to fly down South, with MARS personnel and my brother on board. It was a long and very cold flight and we arrived in Johannesburg amidst some serious thunderstorms, and rushed to Olivedale Clinic. The following morning an orthopedic surgeon, Rob van der Plank, came to see me, ordered more X-rays and had me in theatre by midday. Six hours later I was back in ICU. Somehow, I had hoped to be back home before Christmas but it was only at this point that I suddenly realized how serious the situation was and that I had a very long haul ahead. The surgeon spoke to me at length; I would be lucky to walk again, never mind run, and it was uncertain whether I would have the full use of my left arm again, as the bones in the shoulder were, as he said, "like rice krispies". I was going to need many more operations, a lot of physiotherapy, and a great deal of determination and willpower. It was shattering news; I was a runner, had done two Comrades marathons, and plenty of other runs, and led a very active and independent life. I was now bed-ridden, unable to move much beyond my left leg, and not sure how I was going to get through this.

Christmas 2004 was spent in hospital. My parents returned home and my dear mother came down to South Africa to look after me, as I was allowed out of hospital to stay in the home of good friends, who renovated a whole room and bathroom so that I could stay there. I was able to be lifted into a wheelchair, as long as I kept my right leg in its cast and brace straight. I also had a large black drum-like bag under my left shoulder, which raised the elbow and would hopefully enable it to heal without it locking in one position. All other bones and joints had been pinned with metal rods, plates and screws, including my right hand which needed pins in all the fingers as I had no knuckles left. Physio started and it was TOUGH. At first my physiotherapist did all the movements for me, as I had no muscle tone left, and I was too weak and sore to move. I can remember nights, waiting for the nurses to arrive with a painkiller injection, and crying in agony. Sometimes I didn't think I could go on, and then I would be encouraged by my wonderful family and friends, and I would think of my life before and I'd grit my teeth. I do think that my serious training for running assisted my progress – I had been pretty fit at the time of my accident, and I was also used to punishing my body with some serious training! And I know I had a pretty strong mind to be active again. The determination to run again, never mind walk, was strong.

Weeks went by. I had more operations to "fine tune" the metal pins. When I look back at that time I am not sure how I managed to get through it. When I first came out of hospital, after three months, I could only manage being upright in a wheelchair for short periods, and I was unable to do a thing for myself. I had been "bed bathed" all that time and I can remember my first shower as a moment of extreme bliss. My Mum had to take me to the toilet, and shower me (on a plastic chair under the shower), help me dress and eat, and then on alternate days when I didn't go to the outpatients department for physiotherapy, spend a few hours on physio in the house. I can remember sitting on the dining room table while she worked my right leg – I had to try and bend it once the brace was off. My mother used to try and bend the lower leg by pushing it, and I'd grit my teeth, and both of us had tears pouring down our faces. It was agony. I had to sleep with the shoulder bag under my arm, and then remove that for physio as well. Once I had removable casts I had to start physiotherapy in the swimming pool – an outdoor pool in the garden of the house where we were staying. I knew I had to do exercises in the pool, and even on cold and drizzly days I'd have the wheelchair taken down to the pool so that I could be practically tipped into the water.

I was then allowed to stand upright and use a crutch! It was not easy, as I could not use two crutches because of my broken shoulder, so I used one crutch under my *good* right shoulder and then swivel on my left leg to move. I could not put the right leg down so it was not an easy movement – but one I was determined to master so that I could become more mobile! And with perseverance, I did. I actually moved quicker than people liked me to. Every couple of weeks I had an appointment with the surgeon, and a series of X-rays. My bones were healing very slowly, and I had to have a bone density scan done which showed a very poor result, indicating that I was in a pre-osteoporosis stage. Another worry, but obviously due to the many months of immobility and inactivity. I started on more medication for that, and slowly, with ongoing physio, healing improved.

I shall never forget the day I was told I could stand – unaided – on both legs, and then take a few steps. It sounds like such a minor thing to do but it was miraculous! I confess I was scared, putting all my weight on my right leg, but I didn't collapse. It was an amazing feeling. I remember walking across the room and I actually felt euphoric. Little things like feeling the grass underneath my toes gave me enormous pleasure. All I wanted was to get back to *normal*.

I went back into hospital to have more operations, always a slight set-back as the body adjusts to more antibiotics and surgery, and a period of recuperation. But I persevered with physiotherapy exercises, in and out of the swimming pool, even as the months became colder towards winter. Six months after my accident I was allowed home to Zimbabwe. It was a wonderful day, but strange too, in that I was going back to my *old* life there, without being the same person that I had been before. I felt like I had lost a huge chunk of my life, while everyone else had carried on and I wasn't sure where I was going to fit in. At the time of my accident I had just started a new job, one I was really enjoying, but that had now obviously been taken over by someone else. I wasn't really sure what I was going to, and physically I was not yet strong enough to take on too much.

That was June 2005. From then on, I continued exercising my limbs at home, and I started walking on a treadmill and sitting on an exercise bike at the gym. It was not easy as I still had a lot of pain, but I knew I had to do it. Every three months I travelled to Johannesburg to see my surgeon and have a series of X-rays for him to ascertain how the bones were knitting. By the end of that year I was walking, still with a limp, for five kilometres. It was hard work and sometimes I did despair with the pain, and also the memories of what I used to be able to do. But then I would realize how far I had come, and I was determined to improve. In 2006, I had to have another series of operations, a major one on the shoulder to try and re-align it, which would hopefully assist with its mobility and also reduce the pain, and the removal of some pins in the knee and hand. It was a long operation, and I was back in ICU when my blood pressure dropped critically low. But I rallied, took it easy for a couple of weeks, and was then back home in Zimbabwe, carrying on as before. By the end of 2006, I ran one kilometre for the first time. It wasn't easy as my running gait had totally changed, due to the injuries to my left leg. But it was a wonderful feeling. I was soon running five kilometres, very slowly and not without pain, but it was a *good* pain and I knew that I was strengthening my bones all the time.

In the three years since then a lot has happened in my life. I have married my boyfriend, and we now have a beautiful two-year-old son. He is also a miracle baby; I had been told by specialists in South Africa that it was very unlikely I'd ever be able to have a child. Apart from the fact that my pelvis was out of alignment, the chances of conceiving were minimal as my body's systems had not returned to normal. Well, I proved them wrong! It was a difficult pregnancy, with pain in all limbs, and by the end I was barely able to walk. But baby arrived, strong and healthy and perfect, and I would do it all over again to have him in our lives.

Seven months after his birth my surgeon recommended that I have all the metal pins and plates removed from my arms and leg. So, back to hospital I went leaving my baby with my close friend, who was able to come to South Africa with me and look after him. The operation to remove everything took much longer than expected and it was a grueling five hours before I was back in the ward and awake. Since then I have gone from strength to strength. I can still feel discomfort in some parts of my body which had the most damage, (especially in the winter months!), and my left arm is shorter than my right, but I am alive and mobile. I can now run as far as ten kilometres. I am forever grateful to the wonderful surgeon and medical staff who looked after me throughout, to my beloved family, especially my mother, who were always there with help and encouragement, to my caring husband, and to the many friends and relatives all over the world who kept me in their thoughts and were in contact often.

I would not wish my ordeal on any other person but, for me, it was a turning point in my life and it has honestly made me a better person. I have learned that I am capable of things far beyond my expectations. I now appreciate everything in life so much more, especially the small things. And I also know that the human body is able to cope with amazing adversity, and that things can be overcome with determination and strength of mind.

Julie still lives in Harare, Zimbabwe, with her husband Hilton, and their two-year-old son, Murray. She is working mornings-only in the financial world, and spends the rest of the time looking after her family, running a few times a week, playing and singing with her boy, and walking the dog around the block.

STEVEN DARED TO TURN HIS LIFE AROUND

BY STEVEN SCHARENGUIVEL

Imagine being seven years old again. You're living with your Mother when one day she tells you that she's giving you away. Imagine the impact of knowing that your Mother doesn't want you. I was made a Ward of the State. When I found out I would no longer be living with my mother I became very heartbroken and emotionally distraught and immediately broke down into tears. At the time of the incident it was an extremely painful experience for me because I did not want to become separated from my mother. I cried for days in the hope that I could return to her but eventually had to accept the fact that under no circumstances was the Department going to allow me to go back.

For the next four years I lived in no less than fourteen different homes. The day after I became a Legal Guardian of the State I was placed with my first foster family, an old lady called Marilyn and her middle-aged son called Lesley. At the time that I moved in they both seemed like very nice people since they appeared very sincere and kind towards me. They made a good first impression and provided me with lots of unconditional love and support.

Quickly I realised that what seemed like the perfect family was in fact, a nightmare. Aware that I had significant developmental delays as a result of my autism they took advantage of me by making false accusations about my behaviour and used me to pay for their bills, one being able to afford to smoke a whole pack of cigarettes a day. As a result of this I quickly became recognised as a problem child and was referred to by my Teachers and various Health Professionals as a 'reckless menace'.

I was put on a major sedative medication and when my Mum, who was a Nurse, reported to the Department of Children's Services that the large dosages were likely to have severe psychotic side affects upon me and 'zombie' me out, they simply ignored her.

Being overdosed with medication was reflected in my performance at school. My School Guidance Officer referred to me as a *Drunken Stupor* and summed up my health crisis with the following points:- Slurred speech and language to the extent that speech can be unintelligible; Dribbling; Poor co-ordination and falling over; Lethargy; narrowed sleepy eyes; Wanders around aimlessly; No eye contact; Wanders off while speaking to him; No follow through with instructions; Overall dirty unkempt appearance; Rolled on floor, holding ear and crying; Application to tasks seems severely impaired.

With all this going on, the health professionals from the Mater Children's Hospital and Department believed everything that Marilyn and Leslie said. As a result I was taken advantage of and got into serious trouble for doing and saying things that I was not responsible for. When I look back I don't think my best interests were taken into account nor was I provided with a safe and stable living environment.

According to my mother, Marlene was slightly weird, having had a brain impairment of her own. Her son, Les, who was also intellectually impaired, was Marlene's carer. The Department took them both on as foster carers and it goes to show that DOCS must have missed this in their screening process. Had DOCS identified and become aware of Marlene's and Leslie's problems, they may well have considered cancelling their rights to fostering.

One night after many weeks and months of prayer God reached out to me, and my mother had a dream and said:

"I had a dream that the door closed in on Marlene. I saw the dark-

ness around her, you were crying out for help. I saw Marlene and there was total darkness around her and she was dying of lung cancer. I felt it was because of something I had done, or the way she had behaved that God said, 'All right it is your turn to pass over.'"

Shortly after this, when I was nine years old, Marlene's cancer became critical and my mother's dream came to pass. I was glad to have made it through the ordeal and move on to experiencing a better life.

However, because my stability kept on being broken, as a result of me continually changing foster homes, Schools, Doctors and Child Safety Officers, it made it extremely difficult for me to appropriately manage my behaviour and to be able to exercise control over, and manage my emotions.

All I needed was a sense of stability and to be loved and appreciated by those around me. Unfortunately though, each time things changed I was faced with the added burden of starting my life all over again. In fact, the minute a button was pressed, my emotions would spiral out of control.

After being in a number of different foster homes, a few months before I turned ten, I moved in with the Jenner's who lived in a country town called Beaudesert in the suburb of Rathdowney. They lived in a large spacious house on a five-acre block of land with lots of trees and an open paddock with plenty of room to run around in. They also had a chicken barn with dozens of chickens, a cage full of buggies and a couple of horses.

Rathdowney State School was only a few miles away from where we lived so getting to school was easy. The school was a small one. This made it a lot easier for me to adapt to the school environment and make some new friends.

The Jenner's were different to previous foster families I had lived with. Being their 'first foster child', rather than worrying and condemning me about my problems and hospitalising me, they wanted to see me become happy and successful.

They operated as an authoritarian family and held strict rules that I was encouraged to live up to and maintain. In fact, if I did not follow their rules and obey their orders I would pay the price and receive the consequences. In an effort to make a fresh start I did my best to ensure that I followed their instructions, as I wanted to prove to them that I could be a good person and take full responsibly for my own actions and therefore manage and control my behaviour and emotions well.

While I enjoyed living with the Jenner's I was still trying to come to terms with my past.

Uncle Rodney and Aunty Judy explained:

"You were a good kid but you were quite radical. You could see that you had a nice nature but it wasn't showing because something was affecting it. As soon as you got upset and as soon as you felt your stress level rising, or you were worrying about anything, you could just see you falling off the map. When you got upset everything would become all blurry and you were just off track everywhere. It took us a long time to calm you down. It was a very slow process of calming you down, settling you down and helping you to get back on track. The stuff you experienced was really deep emotional stuff. It was like something of a horror movie where something had really tormented you, that's what it seemed like, that whatever affected you was pretty deep and any little thing would trigger it off."

When I first showed up at the Jenner's house my CSO explained that she worked a lot with me, and that I was a lovely boy and they would have no problems with looking after me.

It was only when my CSO was leaving that she revealed that I had medication that I needed to take. She brought out a Coles bag packed full of medication and since the Jenner's had not been informed about my medical needs they were shocked by the number of medications I required. The bag was three quarters full with ten different varieties of pills and liquids that were meant to be used whenever I experienced any sort of emotional problem. Rodney was especially shocked about the quantity of medicines I had been put on and stated:

"It just seemed to me like you were a guinea pig, that's what it looked like when you showed up at our place with the bag of pills."

The Jenner's could not believe that I needed to take all the medication that I had been given. They did not believe in overdosing me with medication and decided that they would give me an eighth of what I had. They then determined which drugs were most appropriate for me to take and which ones needed to be discarded. The Jenner's believed that it was the medication that caused me to fall asleep in class and what was preventing me from being able to learn, and hence did not believe that it was making any marked difference in my behaviour.

The Jenners decided to stick up for me and approached the health professionals at the Mater Children's Hospital. In their initial efforts they tried to persuade the health professionals into taking me off medication. In spite of what the Jenner's had to say, the health professionals opposed the Jenner's and chose not to acknowledge their views.

Then in an attempt to prove that I did not need medication the Jenner's and my Primary Schoolteacher Mr. Grey teamed up and began to work together on my case. Mr. Grey monitored through the day in the class and kept the Jenners' up to date on how I was going in class with regards to my behaviour and emotions.

The Jenner's, in becoming more aware of my behaviour and how to assist me with resolving issues, began to regularly adjust and change the level of my consumption of medication because they could see that I was not getting results from the medication.

Previously, the health professionals had labeled me.

"We cannot see much of a future for Steven."

"Steven will not be able to live a normal life."

"He will hear voices, and he will be on a lot more drugs than he is now."

"Steven will probably spend the rest of his life in a mental institution."

When the Jenner's mentioned to these health professionals that they had changed the levels of consumption of my medication the doctors went into a mild state of shock and became really angry and upset. This is because in the previous visits they could see a big improvement in me and because of this they thought the bag of medication was the source of my improvement.

The Jenner's went on to tell the health professionals at the Mater that when they monitored me right and I was kept on top of situations, I was in fact:

"A lot better kid off the medication."

In addition Judy said:

"When we started taking medication off him the emotional stuff just stopped."

Unfortunately, as a result the health professionals, in a state of anger and hostility began to lash-out at the Jenner's and decided they would debate against the notion of reducing my medication. Strangely enough the doctors became frustrated with the Jenner's and said:

"What qualifications have you got, how dare you make these decisions?"

After being told off by the health professionals the Jenner's knew they were in trouble. In spite of this, to prove their claim they did a smart thing by bringing my teacher Mr. Grey along to support their claim, as Mr. Grey backed up my big improvement and said:

"Steven has gone from a child in class who could not stay awake, who just couldn't stay on track with his work at all, and has become a kid who is starting to move ahead really quickly."

However here I was, stuck in this tight and cluttered room with little space to move around in and all the health professionals were staring at me expecting me to be normal. Because of the atmosphere I was in I did not act like I did at home and as a result the health professionals couldn't see any improvement. The Jenner's were aware of this and they asked one of the health professionals to take me out into the gardens where the atmosphere was less congested and more open and then watch how I behaved and acted. In spite of this good suggestion the health professionals declined to act in the best interests of me, the child.

The Jenner's did what they believed was the right thing to do even though they knew, it was not necessarily the right thing to do to challenge the authority of a group of health professionals. Not many people will challenge a doctor or a psychiatrist.

These health professionals were trying to feed me medication when all I needed was a little bit of tender love and care and the right surroundings, to give me the chance to successfully rebuild my life. If it wasn't for the Jenner's sticking up for my rights I may not have become the person I am today. I could have easily ended up in a mental institution for the rest of my life.

Thanks to the Jenners, after seven years of medication and behavioural therapy, I never had to take medication again, for they proved the health professionals wrong and changed my life forever. Judy went on to state:

"We felt so proud when Mr Grey went to the hospital with us. We walked out of the hospital feeling as though we had won - that was victory."

Just before I turned eleven years of age, about approximately one year after moving from the Jenners, I moved in with a family that helped me to transform my life forever from the inside-out. Their names were Pam and David. The very first day I met Pam and her son David I was amazed by their patience, calmness, kind-heartedness and their unconditional love. In fact, they were the two most caring persons I had ever met. They made me feel as though I was a prince and that they were my servants that had been called to serve me throughout the course of my foster care journey.

While I had become much more stable after I had moved in with Pam and David, I still had a number of unresolved inner-conflicts that I needed to attend to and deal with. When I first moved in with Pam and her son David they said,

"You were a little lost boy, you were a stranger to us and we were strangers to you. You were lost and you didn't know where you were heading and where you had been. You had no basics. You didn't have a secure home. The people you loved were coming and going. In your previous foster homes you had not been treated well. You couldn't relate to people and you couldn't relate to other children".

This was a result of growing up with mild brain impairment and autism. As a result of this I became an easy target for criticism. Right throughout my primary school years my life was filled with criticism. This made my life miserable. It was hard to enjoy life when students would say things like:-

"You are not smart enough to hang around us."

"You are so dumb; no wonder no one likes you."

"You're a retard and no one hangs around retards."

"You're a crazy bastard."

"You are the biggest loser I know."

"You're hopeless."

"You will never amount to anything."

This is the kind of criticism I had to put up with for the first twelve years of my life. When you think about it, it was no wonder my childhood was so miserable, no one gave me any compliments whatsoever, let alone any hope for the future.

It was only after I had people come into my life that believed in me and encouraged me that I was able to recondition my mind with new and more empowering thoughts and behaviours through the process. This taught me how to not only effectively manage and monitor my behaviours and emotions, but to also compliment and build others up which enabled me to develop a much higher self esteem and become happy and successful.

In their efforts to encourage me whenever I felt down Pam and David would say things like:

"It is not your fault you are the way you are, it is the way you have been brought up. You can't always deal with these problems and it is always going to be really tough for you. Just remember though, you can change if you really want to. There is a way for you to succeed. You just have to keep trying and putting in as much effort as you can. Know that you can only do your best to do what is right, and nothing more. Don't allow other people to control you, do what you believe is right. Try to be good to others and they will attempt to be good back to you. Don't listen to what other people say about you, listen to what you want and do what you want. Prove to people that you can achieve anything if you really want to, you just have to put your mind to it and you will succeed. If you keep trying, sooner or later, you will get somewhere. Be faithful and trust in God and he will show you the way."

During the time I was living with Pam and David, one CSO said:

"We want Steven to build networks, so when he is out of foster care he has people to go too."

My CSO was right, I needed to gain confidence in imitating new relationships, taking risks and at the same time support others while attempting this. If I did not find a way to manage and to build successful relationships then my progress into a healthy independent adult would be jeopardised.

Initially, when I first began to build relationships during my primary school years I struggled. In spite of this, I tried very hard to create friendships with young people my own age around the neighbourhood. It was difficult at first searching the streets for friends however as my confidence grew I formed a number of friendships throughout my primary and high school years with people who had similar interests and before long I had made a number of good friends.

My ultimate way of building relationships occurred through playing sport. Basketball was my most favourite sport and most lunch times I would be playing three on three basketball games with my friends. I was a winner and was known for being a top basketball player. Our school had an outstanding basketball team and I was glad to have captained our team to winning our year ten and year twelve District Basketball Championships.

I took part in the school Cross Country every year and during my final year of school I became the Age Champion for Long Distance Running. Through my dedication to sport during year ten I ended up winning the 2001 School Sportsman of the Year. The deciding factor that won me the award was not just for how good I was and how I played sport, it was my passion for encouraging other members of the team to work together and encourage each other and succeed as a team.

If I wanted to succeed I knew I had to shoot goals while off the court, just as well as I made baskets on the court, if I was going to make it in the game of life. I started to think outside the box and do some new things that I didn't normally do.

I became an active member of my school and my community and now had a dream to become a Life Coach and help others. My efforts began to pay off and by the end of year ten I was considered a top student. Not too long after that I went from being one of the schools worst students to one of their best.

Students within the school, especially those in the lower grades began to look up to me for guidance and direction, so whenever I had the opportunity to provide encouragement, I did. Students and teachers around me began to question me on how I managed to turn my life around so quickly. They were inspired by my change so much so that they continued to encourage me to keep going and follow the school motto *Strive to Excel.*

Outside of school, I went on to do Create Consultant Training with the Create Foundation, a non-government organisation helping to improve the outcomes of children and young people living in foster care. I then became a Create Young Consultant. In this role I was given the opportunity to participate in consultative work with focus groups, public relations strategies with foster carers, department case workers, non-government agencies and others involved with the lives of children; and to provide input into existing policies and practices to assist in the improvement of the processes and practice procedures that govern the Queensland Child Protection system.

In spite all that, the negative, destructive things I had experienced as a kid, at the end of 2003, even with my school being considered one of the worst schools in Queensland, I graduated from Mabel Park High School and during the awards night received an academic achievement award for receiving high achievements in most of my subjects and graduated in the top ten percent of my year level.

In addition to this I also won the Logan Diggers Young Citizen of the Year award for my service to the community and went on to being accepted into Griffith University to do a Bachelor of Human Services with a Major in Community and Family Studies, and successfully graduated in 2007. Aside from this, other awards that I went on to win include The 2004 Logan Diggers Young Citizen of the Year and a Queensland Youth Volunteer Award.

After being held as a ward of the State for a period of eleven years and in my experience as a child protection advocate, I came to know the system from the inside-out. It was therefore no surprise that I became dubbed by professionals working within the child protection system as "the voice for children and young people."

Shortly after becoming a Certified NLP Practitioner inspired by World Number One Peak Performance Coach Tony Robbins, I began to invest most of my time studying the pursuit of human excellence and learnt how to become a Lifestyle Success Coach.

As I became more proficient in my understanding and developed greater confidence within myself I learnt everything there is to know about human excellence and how I could use it to assist other people in not only transforming their lives but also in improving the overall quality of their lives so that they could go on to live a much more satisfying and a more fulfilled life.

As a Lifestyle Success Coach I now run my own Counselling/Coaching practice from home and assist children and young people between the ages of ten and twenty-five who are going through similar experiences to those that I had experienced growing up. I help them in the processes of creating and implementing success strategies which enable them to go on to achieve a well-balanced lifestyle, and maintain optimum health and wellbeing both in the present and the future.

In my efforts to bring my clients to clarity about what success means to them and how to achieve it, I also assist them with developing lifestyle success strategies to help them to overcome any issues to do with organisational management, emotional fitness, relationship building, conflict resolution and health optimisation.

As an accredited life coach Steven helps young adults with similar challenges to his achieve clarity and realise their potential to live a fulfilled life. You can help someone you know achieve this. Steven knows what it's like to be kicked when you're down, but more importantly he knows what it takes to turn it around.

Contact Steven at
steven.s@superself.com.au

SIMONE DARED TO SURVIVE CANCER

BY SIMONE RIDDELL

I considered myself quite a healthy and positive person and learnt the art of *soldiering on* from my amazingly strong and resilient mother and father. Yet I now believe that the few traumas life threw at me in my childhood, adolescence and early adulthood left me more scarred than I realised when I got the diagnosis of cervical cancer at the ripe young age of twenty-eight. I had always focused on carefully looking after my physical fitness, nutritional needs and mental/emotional needs. So, with a diagnosis such as cancer I went through a range of emotions from disbelief, to anger to hopelessness.

I am forever grateful to the doctor who astutely picked up that I hadn't had a pap smear for over five years when I visited her for a prescription for the pill. I hadn't needed to see a doctor for most of my life. It was uncanny that I was getting a prescription for the pill because it was something that I swore I would never take. That was the beginning of the breaking of many rules I had placed on myself.

After receiving the results I was promptly referred on to an oncologist. I was diagnosed and told about the pervasiveness of the disease. The cancer was in the glandular tissue which meant that it was a quick spreading cancer and had a greater chance of spreading to other areas of the body. When I refused treatment, the head of the Royal Brisbane Hospital oncology unit was asked to speak to me and I decided that I wasn't going to let them scare me into their treatment. So in keeping with my *personal rules* or rather *natural code of conduct* I decided not to opt for the recommended surgical treatment and chose to try complementary therapies first. Strangely enough, having surgery was a recurring nightmare that I often had in my sleep and it always ended with me strongly objecting to being anaesthetised.

A pranic healer who told me he had previously been a medical doctor had convinced me that he could heal people with cancer and showed me many a testimonial to prove him. I booked myself in for regular pranic healing treatments and was promised that there was also the option of a new light therapy machine that he had invented which would cure me together with the pranic healing, supplements and strict *anti-cancer* diet he recommended. He gave me research papers about the supplement and had it imported from the USA for me. My diet omitted sugar, most fruits and grains, meat and dairy. I also chose to try homeopathics and did a lot of emotional releasing in relation to sexual abuse incidents from my childhood and adolescence. I even took a three week holiday, which was significant for me because as far as I was concerned, I was too busy running my business to fit cancer into my life.

I could have been judged to be in denial, or avoidance, or just plain gullible, yet I wanted to truly believe in the natural therapies. Not just because it was the nature of my business but also because I wanted to be one of those people who healed myself of cancer as I had witnessed so many other people do in the books I had read and stories I had heard.

Five months had lapsed since my first diagnosis. By this stage I had become quite depressed and teary and was showing the cervical cancer symptoms of spotting, absent periods, fatigue and weight loss, yet that wasn't surprising considering the diet I was on. With the help of an assertive and loving aunt as well as a Kinesiology mentor/teacher, I was able to gain the strength and compassion for myself to go back to a doctor and be re-tested. I cut my losses with the Pranic Healer and didn't bother to chase him for any of the promises he had failed to deliver.

I was referred to a gynaecologist who booked me in for surgery the very next day. I was lucky to have three amazing girlfriends present at the appointment. They were my most long standing friends who I had completed my nursing degree with and helped guide me to consent. I was finding many excuses to put off having the surgery. I had clients booked in and had promised to help my boyfriend Phil with our move to the Sunshine Coast. My wonderful friend Anna stopped me in my tracks and told me with consternation and sternness,

"Simone, you have cancer and you need to get it treated. Your work and Phil's needs don't matter at the moment."

I had been told. There was no way I could back out. From there cascaded a series of three surgeries, an MRI and the removal of lymph nodes and a modified hysterectomy and exploratory surgery of the pelvic and abdominal regions. In this process I discovered that my health insurance didn't cover hospital insurance. The urgency of the matter meant that choosing the expensive private option was better than waiting for the public option.

The first surgery removed the tumour in two sections. It was uncertain whether it was one big tumour or two smaller ones, therefore the gynaecologist had to refer me to an oncologist. Due to this fact and the fact that I had enlarged lymph nodes on the MRI, I was advised to have a hysterectomy and went about grieving and mentally preparing myself for losing my uterus and the ability to have children. Upon returning to the oncologist I was told that he had discussed my treatment with a number of specialists in Brisbane and had reconsidered the hysterectomy. Due to the fact that I hadn't had children, and perhaps also the tears and shock I had demonstrated, the procedure was going to be modified to remove the cervix and join the uterus to the vagina.

I continued to see clients and operate business as normal, even up until my second surgery. After that I realised that I wasn't going to be able to continue. My energy was waning and I felt I needed to retreat to living with my parents on the family farm near Goondiwindi. My will was to continue seeing my Goondiwindi clients and have more time for myself and my healing. My purpose for carrying on in this way and focusing on my work was fuelled by my passion for Kinesiology and KaHuna massage. I had witnessed so many amazing results and built such precious relationships with my clients. My grand vision to be an inspiration to people by continuing my work despite adversity also stoked my determination to continue. It had been an extremely challenging and upsetting thing for me to have to refer all the clients I had been seeing in Brisbane. I didn't want to let go of my Goondiwindi clients as well. So despite the physical pain and drain that I still felt from the cancer treatment, I continued practicing in my business. The focus I had on my beloved kinesiology and massage practice also helped me to deal with the relationship break-up that I had been through while having treatment for cancer. Yet little did I know that I wasn't out of the woods yet.

The day I got the news that the clinic I was now working from had been destroyed by fire was quite surreal. I had only been back in my practice for a week and had so lovingly and whole-heartedly established stocks, certificates and equipment in this place, without yet having transferred my business insurance I might add. This meant another huge financial and emotional loss for me. With this solemn news, I became immersed in a gamut of emotions and thoughts for days and weeks thereafter. It began with a mental inventory of the tangible losses of stocks, tables, pictures, certificates, books, linen, client records etc. Then emerged the intangible losses such as my sense of self and the ten years of my life I had spent building the business. It then took a winding trip of highs and lows which looked something like…

"I was too tired to come back to work anyway, great that I can have more rest."

"I was angry and resentful about thankless tasks in having to run a business anyway. What a perfect time in my life to have a change. I can get a stable income working for someone else and have less responsibility. No responsibility, hooray, I can travel anywhere now."

"But what about the last ten years of my life and income that I have invested in this business? I now have nothing to show for it. How could I possibly give up on this investment? How can I say goodbye to all those clients and let them all down? What are they going to think of my giving up so easily?"

Once the head chatter subsided, the cold hard emotions set in. I felt complete loss and for what seemed like hours and hours and days and days, I cried. My tears were not only for my loss, but also the losses from my whole life, and then the losses of the whole world. The story running through my head was "we enter into this world and from day one we are given so much. We are gifted with objects, people, experience, relationships, money etc. etc. And then at some time throughout life we lose it or we die".

I prayed that I could see life differently and that I could be supported and encouraged in life. I had just read a book called *Boundless Love* which gave me advice that, if I connected with this place of boundless love inside me, I could survive more hopefully. So I wrote and I painted and I swam with affirmations and mantras circling around my head. Amidst the darkness and tears I was feeling, I also felt a mystical sense of nurturing, comfort and some degree of joy.

2007 now represents the most turbulent year of my life, and the cancer seemed like the easiest part to deal with. It was clearly treatable and there were so many movements of love directed my way. By surrendering to the process I was able to experience so much love and support from so many people, friends, family, professionals and acquaintances. I didn't have to do anything to be worthy or loved. I felt like a sick, sorrowful, needy person and I was feeling more loved than ever before.

And from then on a string of events occurred. A compassionate stranger, who was a friend of a friend, continued to call me and allowed me to listen and speak in a way which reminded me of who I am and what I value. He lived in Brisbane and eventually I found myself back in Brisbane in the presence of a passionate romance which has since blossomed into a deep and wholesomely supportive relationship. He has been very patient with me while I was at my emotional worst! It was very difficult for me to talk about and face my losses and my grief which put me in a difficult space sometimes. I had thrown all my dreams and visions for my business and myself out the window as they were also a painful topic for me to confront. Tears and diversions were becoming my survival tool. I found myself becoming very busy much of the time to help me to avoid the emotional pain, as well as the pain that I was still feeling physically from the surgeries.

With my intentions to integrate back into life and *soldier on* I got myself employed with Health by Design. My role involved conducting workshops and coaching people with their health and manual handling in workplaces. In this period I travelled every month, which I loved at first as it allowed me to see my family out west and visit the beaches on the New South Wales coast. Yet my spirit and body were becoming more and more depleted.

Eighteen months on from the fire and that huge loss of will and passion for life, I got to that same place again where I felt I had done all I could to recuperate, and to no avail. I had taken some time out, had kinesiology, homeopathy and acupuncture for healing and engaged myself in employment with a wonderful bunch of people who I shared many laughs and smiles with. Yet deep inside, I felt completely washed out and empty. I was exhausted and couldn't stop the tears that would come most days. I could no longer trust my body to perform as it was constantly dealing me heaviness in my movements, tears in quiet moments and headaches and migraines at the end of each working week. Loss of memory and concentration was something that I battled with ever since the third surgery. This didn't help my trust and belief in me either, especially considering I had been complimented so often for my great memory and focus previously.

To the outside world I was projecting a highly capable and confident and sociable being. My inner world was in conflict to this and I felt that I couldn't cope with life anymore. I kept pushing myself to live out my life as a fully functional, sociable and happy person. I realised in hindsight that by doing this, I was simply burning energy that I didn't have. So again, I turned to the medical world. My blood tests were all clear for any iron, B vitamin, thyroid or kidney deficiencies so I continued on telling myself that everything was fine. When I couldn't take the pain of exhaustion and depression anymore, I did my research with friends about the experience of taking antidepressants and went back to my doctor to enlist the support of antidepressants and psychology consultations. I think this has been one of my greatest choices as it has allowed me to drop some of the *busy and anxious tendencies* I have had in relation to compulsively getting things done.

My psychologist has been wonderful in helping me to put my life into perspective and so I have been able to let go enough to rest some more and take the brave journey of looking within again. I realised that I had abandoned all my dreams, and I had let go of my urge to be the inspiration of overcoming adversity. In my opinion, the life that I was leading was merely an empty existence of putting on a brave face to slot into the hum drum physical world. When I began filling myself with inspiring reading and self nurturing practices, I regained hope and will to live more fully. I have been able to restructure my life to focus on the things that I more truly want to pursue rather than simply 'survive a harsh and painful world'. I found again my ability to dream and be motivated to act on these dreams to further strengthen myself and create the life I wanted to live. I have decreased my workload and am more at peace with allowing myself to have 'off' days. My business is slowly starting to build again and this is just perfect for me now.

Since having to rebuild my self esteem, strength and passion for life, I have now also had the chance to re-master my business. With a renewed appreciation for the business of Kinesiology and Massage I have enjoyed the opportunity to rebuild my business with greater mindfulness. The business I now call *Heaven and Well* has a focus on Life Support: Physically, Mentally and Emotionally. My life experience tends to be naturally attracting people who are seeking support in dealing with life changes or recovering from injuries and illness. The business name *Heaven and Well* was chosen with the help of my loving and encouraging partner Brian, who is quite the word wizard! This appeared to be the perfect business name as it captures some common goals we have in life, that being peace, joy, love and health. All of these I believe to be truly valuable in life, and something which Kinesiology and KaHuna help to achieve. *Heaven and Well* also depicts the essence of our highest potential and the inner well of resources, which we can all access with a little help!

For more information you are welcome to
phone me on 0427 320 302, or visit www.heavenandwell.com

Many Blessings, Simone Riddell.

STACEY DARED TO COPE DIFFERENTLY

BY STACEY HUISH

Hi, this chapter is all about coping and, of course, about switching your attitude. The story shared here is raw for a reason. I want you to get the impact your attitude plays on your life. I hope that I can get the message across to you.

The Build Up

Nineteen years had passed so far, and the only thoughts going through my head were how much life sucked! Yes that is right! You heard me, I said it SUCKED! Hatred was bestowed upon everyone and everything. What had brought about this attitude of Hatred towards everyone and everything was this:-

The only style of communication I knew throughout childhood was based upon a lot of sarcasm, put down humour, never fully listening to what the other person was saying, and never expressing how I truly felt about anything. This so called 'normal' way of speaking was used on numerous occasions, in many different situations. After speaking this way, feelings of fear and anger would engulf me as I knew things had been made worse. Underlying problems were never dealt with directly and lots of things were totally ignored. Conclusions were formed even when all the facts were not presented. Frustrations escalated as misinterpretations and misunderstandings of what was being said took place. There was a lot of unexpressed conflict.

At this point my huge apparent dislike for this way of speaking became very clear and I started to try many good intentioned social experiments to meet my needs. The journey to feel understood and to have full comprehension of what the other person was telling me had begun. The experiments started with my messages being repeated in broken record style, or changing the words used to express the message differently. The challenge was finding a way to get someone to listen to me. I still did not feel understood, and I definitely did not feel listened to.

Refusing to accept failure at this point, the journey continued. I needed to know I got their *truth* of their message. I started repeating back what the other person said in a parroting style and sometimes paraphrased fashion. Usually their responses were, “No, that’s not what I said at all! You just don’t listen! You don’t understand me!” and then they usually left the room. Feeling defeated and discouraged I gave up because those attempts were complete failures. None of them worked. The only things that were created were more bottled up feelings of frustration and anger.

Fed up with everything, I made a decision to simply stay silent. At a very young age child logic had been used to conclude that I could not get hurt anymore if I did not speak anymore. Decisions had been made that any laughter, putdown humour, and sarcasm of being silent could be tolerated, but never the crushing of my own dreams and life choices.

Staying silent is not recommended as it causes problems of its own. Generally silence as a communication tool results in short word phrases being used as responses, such as “Sure. Yes. Maybe. No. Whatever you want.” And these one word replies really do stop the flow of conversation from going anywhere, usually causing more frustrations and more conflicts for both parties.

What an Attitude!

Completely Numb to Everything

A young girl who was very ANGRY, very depressed and very

suicidal. At the time, I was living in a share house, working full time waiting tables at night and studying business management during the day, was president of the Student Representative Council (SRC) and had a boyfriend, thinking that having a relationship would make everything all better.

On the outside this life looked to everyone else like it was the best thing in the world... but on the inside, the heart, the soul and the emotions were completely screwed up... hearing everyone saying how incredible my life was... and that they wished that they could do what I do, juggling so many things. But no one, not a single person actually spent any time at all, getting to know or to understand. They only wanted to see what they wanted to see, the outside things, all the activities that were taking place. According to them I was okay and they could be okay with me if all these things were taking place. Everyone had always said that if you are doing all these things, working a job, studying to better yourself, and had a boyfriend, then you were happy... They were totally wrong and so far from the truth!

Right up until this point in life, all the anger, hurt, unasked questions, embarrassments, fears and anxieties had been stuffed inside and held down. It was literally like being a champagne bottle, completely full to the brim and having no room for anything more. The cork was on... and the whole bottle was being shaken up... Now you know what happens to a bottle of champagne when it gets shaken, that's right, the cork comes flying off and the liquid sprays out everywhere.

This was the point that I was at.

Nineteen years of totally unexpressed emotions, nineteen years of unexpressed pain and hurt, nineteen years of unexpressed anger, nineteen years of unexpressed everything! I was a ticking time bomb going through life with absolutely no coping skills.

Then came the offering... Drugs! Boy oh Boy oh Boy! This was the best thing in my life at the time. This drug, marijuana, was powerful and the discovery was used to numb every part of me to the point where I could not feel anything anymore. I could not feel the pain, I could not feel the hurt, and I could not feel the ANGER! I could not feel the world. I was numb, I was completely and totally numb. I could now function in the world with everything that I had to do without feeling it. There was no feeling anymore. I could now cope.

Every morning before flinging the covers and getting out of bed, the drug would be consumed... just so the events of the day could be coped with. Then throughout the day, several times a day in fact, more consumption of the drug, always topping up when the effects were wearing off. In between the business management classes the drug was taken so that the afternoon classes were able to be coped with. Always having more of the drug just before work so the stress of waiting tables was able to be coped with, and consuming even more of the drug just before going home to the share house so that the housemates could be coped with.

The numbness had taken effect BUT, the hatred was still being bestowed upon everyone, and everything and that included me. Yes! I hated me too. And all this ANGER and hurt, and pain was still inside. It was stuck there. The numbness may have taken hold, but the ability to cope was still a mystery. All of the stuff being held onto and none of that stuff inside was coming out.

I was coping in the best way that I knew how to at the time.

Dying and Being Reborn

Every day upon waking, the only constant thoughts running through the head were all about how I wanted to die and be reborn.

I thought that if I could just die and get out of here, and then be reborn again, then I could start my life over and learn all the things that I really needed to learn as a kid. I knew that I would have to teach myself everything that I needed to know.

Every second of everyday, the thoughts were the same. Always, over and over and over and over again, "I just want to die and be reborn".

It was the end of semester, handing in the last assignment meant the whole course was now finished and graduation would be soon. Leaving the office and walking down the long corridor, I started to look like Quasimodo as all of the pain took over, making my body double over and hardly able to walk. I got into the car and drove home. The next day lying on the floor, unable to move with continual vomiting, the hospital was the only choice. Upon arrival, the staff did tests and pronounced me clinically dead on arrival. The doctors were stunned as to how I was even alive. My entire body had shut down completely, except for three organs which continued to work. The heart, lungs and brain. And that was it. Every other organ had swollen so big that it just shut down and stopped working. I had had tonsillitis for over three months untreated, over six months of glandular fever and second stage pneumonia. I really should have been dead.

The drug at the time had done its job really well, while completely numb to the whole world, and to everyone in it, I was also completely numb to myself and to my bodies signals. All the symptoms that had emerged, the sore throat, the coughing, etc had been ignored because they were the same symptoms as when taking drugs.

I had died… I got exactly what I had thought about each and every day. I got what I wanted.

I lay there in bed not being able to move. If I wanted to move my finger, I had to get a person, who was not me, to come over to me and pick it up and move it for me. In fact I had to do that for every part of my body, arms, legs, everything. I would look at the orange juice on the table and wonder why I was not picking it up to drink, I was thirsty, but my arm was not getting that orange juice.

The doctor said to me it would be one month before I would be sitting up in bed, three months before I could walk again and twelve months before I would be going back to any kind of work.

The doctors had put me on a drip to get antibiotics into me. Once the drip had come out, I absolutely, flat out, refused any and all medication while in the hospital.

I knew that the only organ that was working in my body was my brain. So, every day I visualised myself on the operating table and the doctors cutting me open and cutting out the bad swollen, sick organs and throwing them in the bin and getting brand new healthy ones and sewing them into me and then stitching me back up. I did this every day, several times a day for about TWO weeks until I was well enough to go home.

Within one month of *dying* I was back on my feet and taking dance classes once a week. The rest of the time I would sleep anywhere between twenty and twenty-two hours a day. I would only get up on Wednesday at about four in the afternoon, have a shower and go to the dance class and then come home and sleep the rest of the week. I did not eat or shower.

One Sunday brought about a change. A chance meeting with a lady who did re-birthing led to ten re-birthing sessions being completed. Each one represented the nine months in the womb and the tenth was coming down the birth canal and being born.

I was reborn. I had got what I had been thinking about… I got my wish. I had now died and been reborn, just exactly as I had thought about it, each and every day.

New Beginnings

Now, life was beginning again! The journey of teaching me everything that I needed to know started. Longing to understand and wanting to know everything, steps were taken one at a time, arriving at many different classes and courses along the way. Meeting people from all walks of life helped me to grasp worlds that I never knew existed.

The first course attended was *What is Anger? And how do you manage it!* Because anger was a complete and total mystery and there was a long standing hurt, needing to be heard was really important. The lessons learnt were all about how to express anger in a way that is healthy and without hurting the other person. This process started to empty out the champagne bottle, and a different kind of normal emerged.

The hunger for learning and the thirst for knowledge continued for many years. The next course I attended was "How to communicate, how to talk to another person that was positive and supportive and encouraging".

Throughout these learning stages, electrifying excitement and a huge sense of relief welled in me as it became apparent that all of those experiments that were tried time and time again were not complete failures after all. They were just incomplete responses. An inner knowing had led me down the right track all along. The right path had been explored from the beginning.

Learning took place and discovery lead to realization that all of that paraphrasing, saying back in my own words the feelings and information from what I heard the other person say is a skill called *Reflective Listening.*

More learning uncovered that the repeated broken record attempts to get my own messages across was an incomplete "I Message." These "I Messages" are made up of feelings and how another person's behaviour actually affects you. When *Reflective Listening* and "I Messages" are combined and used correctly, they create a very powerful synergy creating a sense of understanding, feeling listened to and keeping conversation flowing.

Everything had worked during the learning stages and now curiosity beckoned to see it work for real. Definitely willing, eager, and able to give this new found knowledge a go, feelings of strength and safety rushed through me like electricity as I stepped out into the world.

The Attitude Has Changed!

With new found knowledge it was so much easier to enter into many different situations with grace, ease and a knowing that I can do this. I can clearly state what I want or need to say without fears of being misunderstood.

Previous frustrations have been eliminated, and my self-confidence is building more and more. Misunderstandings and misinterpretations are now a thing of the past, and there is a freedom all of its own, when people feel listened to and understood by me. Knowing how to feel listened to by others is an absolute blessing, and the only experiments that I now do are in the science lab - not in conversations with people.

A multitude of different courses followed. All of these courses, presented new skills and new ways of coping… Finding these other ways has been a true blessing, so much better than the coping mechanism the drugs gave me at the time. They never taught me how to cope, they never gave me any skills of dealing with anger, or how to talk to another person or how to get your needs met.

Once I had learnt skills of coping, how to express anger, and all the other emotions in a healthy way the drugs just left my life in an instant. They were no longer part of my everyday existence and I didn't need to numb myself anymore. Learning that there were other ways to deal with situations has given the gift of safety and trust, where I now feel things: I feel joy, I feel happiness, I feel authentic, I feel real, I feel life and I feel like living!

Many years later, a meeting with a business coach took place, whereupon the coach started asking questions. He had failed to find out the whole story before passing judgment. He had heard me say to him, "I used to take drugs!" and from those few words, he judged me to be a drug addict, insisting that I admit what he only wanted to hear *that I was a drug addict.*

I said to this person, that I would tell him the truth, if he was ready to hear my truth!

I said this - "A long time ago, I was a very angry young girl with no coping skills, and I had found something that numbed the pain and allowed me to cope with everyday life. Until such time that I had learnt a new way of coping, and then the drugs just left my life, I no longer needed them anymore, I was coping in the best way I knew how to at the time."

I urge you to get to understand another person first before you pass judgement on them. Because like me, they are probably doing the best that they know how to do with whatever information they have, and coping in the only way that they know how to at the time.

Where hatred was, love has blossomed, I genuinely feel Love for myself, I authentically Love the life I am living now. There is a real Love for the people in my life and for the things that I am doing. And most of all I LOVE teaching others communication skills that allow them to get their needs met.

Love your life, Love Yourself and LOVE your Attitude!

Stacey Huish is a published author, trainer, seminar presenter, business and Life Coach, and public speaker. Stacey has inspired many different people to make positive changes in their own lives through the use of effective communication skills. She provides the paradigm shift for the way people communicate with each other. To download her Free Report, “Tips on Effective Communication Skills”, please visit

www.Only-Effective-Communication-Skills.com.

TRACY DARED TO FULFILL A PROMISE

BY TRACY EATHER

"When *we grieve there is no right way or wrong way. There is just your way, so if it's your way then it's the right way for you."*

Hi, my name is Tracy Eather and I am privileged and honoured to be asked by Diane Carter to give my story for her book, thank you so much Di, it's also an honour to come to know you as a friend.

I lost my daughter Amanda Jean Carter to the insidious disease *melanoma* the most deadly form of skin cancer! Here is Amanda's and my journey taken from our website.

Amanda Carter, *my darling beautiful daughter,* touched the hearts of so many people in her life. At just twenty-five she lost her brave battle with *melanoma cancer* on the 12th of November 2007.

Just two years before Amanda had noticed a change in a mole on her back; it had become red and itchy. After consulting her GP the mole was excised and came back *Stage Two Melanoma*, so more was to be cut away and this was given the all clear. Only a few months later at her regular Mole Screening appointment it was revealed that she should have more cut away. Again, this also was given the all clear.

In June 2006, Amanda felt three small lumps in her back about five centimetres away from where her mole was removed, diagnosis

– *Stage Three Melanoma* - (metastatic *melanoma).*

The lumps were cut out as was a section under her left arm where it was discovered that four of the lymph nodes were infected with *melanoma* cells.

"This is serious!" were the fading words of her doctor. Serious did not explain that we would not have Amanda with us this Christmas; the reality, totally incomprehensible!

Amanda actually recovered really well from *that* surgical invasion, had a beautiful and healthy family holiday at Burleigh Heads on the Gold Coast Christmas 2006.

Amanda felt her life was now falling back into place. She was accepted at University to do a Bachelor of Education and planned to work part time while performing her important role of full time mother and wife. Then in January 2007, she thought she just had a groin injury from crouching down to be with her little boy, then only two years old. After unsuccessful chiropractic and physiotherapy sessions it wasn't until March 23rd that her *melanoma* specialist discovered that Amanda had a nine centimetre tumour in her left hip and socket. Surgery at first was out of the question but after eight sessions of radiotherapy, surgery then became an option. On 7th June 2007 Amanda had a full left hip replacement and reconstruction, something that is usually associated with the older generation.

We were told that in just a few short weeks she would be on her feet again without the crutches or wheel chair, something she worked so determinedly at. Then Amanda was experiencing back pain which was put down to the imbalance associated with limping for so many months, unfortunately this was not the case and getting back on her feet was not to be. Another scan with doctors at the Princess Alexandra Hospital found another tumour on her L4 vertebrae, as well as spots on her spleen. Again more radiotherapy, this time prescribed for pain relief.

Unfortunately relief from pain did not eventuate for Amanda, my brave girl. This strong and determined woman still was not giving in. She quietly suffered the excruciating pain until her twenty-fifth birthday on August 19th, she was not going to be in hospital for her birthday! We admitted her to the Wesley Hospital for pain relief and pain control on the evening of the twentieth via ambulance to the emergency department of the Wesley hospital.

This time, scans discovered that her excruciating pain was related to a fracture of her L4 vertebrae (second vertebrae from the bottom of the spine). Little wonder why her prescribed drugs were not working effectively, the fracture was pressing against the spinal cord and nerves. I don't think we could even comprehend the pain she was tolerating silently and bravely. Doctor's orders were *no movement* because of possible irreversible damage to her spine and paralysis from the waist down. Spinal surgery was the next step; her L4 was removed and replaced.

We all took this on as being what had to be done, the actual seriousness and urgency was again incomprehensible. It was what had to be done to get Amanda back on her feet, her goal, so she could get to that beach holiday that is planned each year at Christmas. Again we believed that she would be on her feet in just a few weeks.

It was during this month long stay in hospital that the media was showing Claire Oliver's plea for Solarium closures. As solariums may not be directly to blame, Amanda's voice, now through me, is *"that if there is even the slightest chance, why risk it"*.

Amanda did use the solarium under the age of eighteen, and again several sessions before her wedding day. AND her skin type was not checked according to regulations. She had very fair and burn easily skin (Type One) and should have been advised NOT to use the solarium especially without consent.

We contacted *60 Minutes* after Claire's story and *A Current Affair* took on Amanda's plea *(*aired 18th September*)*. Amanda returned home with the belief and hope, that she would wean off her Grasbey automatic pump that injects pain relief drugs, *morphine!* and get back on her feet so she could go and enjoy that beach holiday she had booked for December 6th.

Four short weeks later on 16th October we had Amanda back in hospital for pain control again as her prescription just was not working for her. The weeks to follow were just a blur, numbness invaded us deeper. We went in thinking at very first that she would be able to get out for her holiday even for a few days was the aim, it very quickly came to realization that she most likely wasn't going to get out of hospital, wasn't going to see her beautiful son James' third birthday on 2nd December, wasn't going to get out to enjoy that beach holiday and wasn't going to get out and see Christmas, her most favourite time of the year.

How do you celebrate and bring forward her son's birthday and Christmas so that she was able to enjoy these days when it wasn't the real dates, how do you manage to be happy in doing that, how do you watch this brave person, a part of you, who enjoyed life to the maximum, made everything important and count, achieve and accomplish more than a lot of us today, fade away so quickly in those last few weeks before your very eyes?

My darling beautiful girl just amazed us, and the palliative care team, with her dignity, the sheer determination and the tower of strength that took her through to the last days of her life, days that extended way past her time they gave her. During her last few conscious days I promised her that I would be her voice and grant her wish for Melanoma Awareness, that it is not "just" a skin cancer that can be cut away, it can invade the body aggressively in any of the organs or bones. In Amanda's case it was first her hip, then her spine. She had the hip replacement on June 7th and spinal surgery on Aug 27th. THAT'S how AGGRESSIVE it was for her, now she is gone! I promised Amanda that she was not going to go through all this horrific pain and parting this world, as we know it, so soon, for nothing. Melanoma *is* ***SERIOUS*** and does take people's lives, young lives, aggressively, painfully and quickly!

People constantly say to me "how can you be so strong" or "how are you handling this so well?" My answer to this was that I have to, I have to be strong. Yes I am numb, but just very recently I did come to the realisation as to how I was helped being kept strong – it's because of the valued support group around me, family, friends, nurses, doctors, acquaintances, everybody in their own way held out a hand of support, prayers, hope and encouragement. And now my aim, with the help of my family, friends and hopefully the community, is to set up a foundation in Brisbane in honour of Amanda's bravery and wishes, so donations can be used for Melanoma Awareness. The big picture, education vans visiting high schools, starting with hers, and community groups etc armed with the information and skin scanners. This project, my promise to her, is what will also help me get through this!

Amanda has left behind a devastated community of broken hearts, her husband Jay, her beautiful son James, her Dad Rhett and her brothers Brendan and Michael, me, her numb but determined Mum, and so many more people who came to love such a beautiful soul, who is so sadly missed!

My darling girl, I will be your voice and your wish will become your Legacy.

This story was written within weeks of Amanda's passing, looking back now I really don't feel much different, yes I am stronger and my mind a little clearer, but the reality of having my twenty-five year old daughter taken away from me so horrifically hits me some days so unexpectedly. Just recently Amanda's ashes were stolen in a burglary at her husband's home. Her ashes and personal belongings, jewellery, photos, and a special DVD that she had made for her son days before her parting were kept securely in a safe. This safe along with other things were stolen, I bet the thieves thought they had a treasure… yes our treasure; her husband's married life memories and her son's mementos. I thought I was okay with this but looking back, yes I had a blurred week or so. I look at my grandson today thinking he is starting prep school next year, without his mum seeing his first day, without him having his mum at his side on his first day. This little boy's normal life is a life now without his mum and to try and understand why the other children have their mums constantly around. I always say, and he knows that, if there was ever a mother in this world that loved their child the most, it was Amanda. She was so in love with her beautiful boy, she cherished the ground he walked on, she made absolutely every minute of every day about James. She nurtured, she cared, and she even felt his pain.

We don't know the answer as to why Amanda was only with us for such a short time, but while she was here she achieved and accomplished more than a lot of us today. She has shown us all the dignity, the sheer determination and the tower of strength proven throughout her life, and while she went through the journey she undertook with the cancer melanoma.

From her strength and witnessing the pain she suffered, I am making good on my promise to her and have set up the Melanoma Awareness Foundation (MAF) with a good friend and Business partner Deb Masterton. The Foundation is dedicated to the increased protection and preservation of you and your family's skin. Through fundraising, community and corporate support, MAF's aim is to save lives through improved awareness and education programs. We want to assist as much as possible with projects to change current behavioural attitudes by increasing awareness through prevention methods for melanoma and skin cancer.

We have successfully been involved with the Sunwise Safety Campaign in January 2008; the Solarium Regulation changes along with our local MP Michael Choi, and the Queensland Government's Skin Cancer Prevention Health Promotion Unit launch of *Under The Queensland Sun* 5 year strategic plan at the end of last year.

We do have several fundraisers throughout the year, our biggest presently being MAD March (Melanoma Awareness Day) held on the 1st Sunday of March every year.

So, how do I *stay positive* and *on top of things?* My boys Brendan, Michael (sons) Jay (son-in-law), James (Amanda's baby), and my beautiful granddaughter that I don't see very often, but think of nearly every day, too - Angelina Jean! And of course, my busy volunteer work for this amazing Foundation that was set up in February 2008 *"In Loving Memory of Amanda Jean Carter."* How do I do this? This comes I think from the inner strength powered with my knowing that Amanda's Spirit is always with me and I have to now do or carry on her strengths and beliefs, and help instill these in *her* family so that this part of her never *dies*!

This is *my family*, this is my strength, and I don't have my family network around me for support, I don't have the bond with my mother that I had/have with Amanda, we were/are so close and got closer each day as she matured into a beautiful young mother herself, the bond that I have always longed for as long as I can remember and still longing for now with my own mother.

From her first smile at three weeks, to her last smile after her last breath. She looked so beautiful, she is so beautiful. I love her so very, very much and miss her every moment of the day.

"In memory of You"
The memory of your face,
Your smile,
Your giggle,
Your open loving heart,
We will remember fondly,
As we say our goodbyes,
To a beautiful soul,
Who radiated brilliance
In so much - as a smile!

Thank you Di, for allowing me to express this again for people to share, as the more I talk about it the more I am hoping people will get a better understanding of melanoma and what it can do, not only taking away a precious young life, but also realise the enormous effect it has on those that are left behind.

And if anyone wishes to help with fundraising *(we'd love it if someone or a group could do the fundraising so we can concentrate on the Awareness and Education part)* or to donate to the Foundation please contact me on the details below.

Tracy Ann Eather

Love The Skin You're In!

®

Protect and Nurture!
Office: 1300 852 546
Fax: 1300 852 786
Web: www.melanomaawarenessfoundation.org.au
Email:info@melanomaawarenessfoundation.org.au
Email: tracy@melanomaawarenessfoundation.org.au
PO Box 5109, Alexandra Hills, Qld 4161

BRIAN DARED TO CLIMB MOUNTAINS

BY BRIAN HUACK

Way back in the early 90's I realized there was something wrong with my sight, noticing it when I was driving home after work late each evening, I felt the street lights should not look as they did. Also, reading the picking order forms at the warehouse at work was becoming more and more difficult each week.

The day I realized I had to step over the line and visit an optometrist, wasn't an easy one. Safety for other people, especially due to my driving, was always on my mind. I was a labourer, for cryin' out loud. All I knew was how to use my hands, lifting, driving a forklift, driving a car, using spanners, reading order forms. The stigmatism around wearing glasses still burned in my mind from when I was a child. School kids are like that.

Not only did I find out I needed glasses, the optometrist suggested I visit an ophthalmologist.

'Huh! There's a difference?'

How many questions go through your head? I can't remember how many went through mine at the time. I was always a labourer, up to my elbows in grease, especially at the weekends. Two months later, after a raft of tests, my specialist gave me the news.

"Sit down; I have something to tell you!" I was going blind… with a condition called Retinitis Pigmentosa. I describe it as having billions of stars and a bad fog impairing my vision. Imagine having your head in the thickest part of the Milky Way with your eyes open or closed. My retinas were deteriorating.

I was twenty-six years old, for crying out loud, and had plenty of life in front of me. I had a driver's license, forklift ticket and a love of machinery. Cars were one of my loves as well, especially the V8's. That doesn't mean I don't have a love of V8's now, it just means that all I can do is listen. It's very frustrating to hear and not see!

Life began to go through a few changes. Don't even mention the Sunday Paper. The last day I could read the paper I spent three hours by myself, with no distractions, and would have read half a dozen articles, virtually letter by letter, then went to sleep exhausted.

Realising that communication through letters would become a hassle, finding a job was the next challenge. Understanding that what I could do previously has nothing to do with what I was now able to achieve after losing my sight. This is where I also had to take the step over the line and learn a new talent. That was learning the computer and touch typing. This was a big step to take, considering what my thoughts on a computer when I had sight were, that they were a TV screen with a keyboard attached and they would not amount to much. Please don't get me wrong I was, at the time, thinking like the majority. However, thankfully, I discovered that they amounted to much more. These days, I can't go too long without checking emails or checking out the internet.

I first had to take the step across the line and ask for a White Cane around mid-2001. This was a seriously hard decision for me, as I felt having a white cane would be a great neon sign telling people to stay away. I felt the cane would bring the wrong attention to me. I was a person who at that time didn't like to attract attention, or be noticed for the wrong reasons.

For me to gain confidence in using the cane, I had to wait until around the middle of January 2002. The day started as usual. I was sitting in the sun eating breakfast when something made me realize that the sun was up. I then realized that the sun would be up the next day and the next, and so on. That evening I went out with the cane extended to a 'Blues Venue' under the Storey Bridge. I then found out that people didn't care that I had a cane. People spilled my beer as much as anyone else's. From that time onwards I had the confidence to have the cane extended each time I went anywhere and walked with my head up.

Joining a martial arts group in late 2001 also gave me the confidence to walk anywhere I wished. I felt this was very important, due to the stigma surrounding most blind people, who are afraid to get out and enjoy the wider world more presented for the sighted. Holding my head high and with a slight grin I think let me into, and around, most areas in which some sighted people are cautious. Joining Toastmasters gave me the ability to speak to either a group of people or in a one on one situation.

I joined the business club SWAP in Brisbane and found out that those people didn't worry either, as at the end of the breakfast, most of the people who attended did not place their chairs back under the table, which was rather painful for the shins, keep in mind these parts of my body are attached to my brain. When I don't use the cane correctly I get a sudden reminder.

I even receive comments on how people forget that I am vision impaired and the funny thing is, I forget myself sometimes.

I feel the journey I have had to trek so far has given me the ability to look for opportunities, both personal and professional. I believe that if I hadn't lost my sight, I would not have had half of the experiences I have taken on, including looking for business opportunities, and the personal growth challenges I have encountered.

In March of 2009, I joined a group on a 'Determination Walk' up to the summit of Mount Kilimanjaro, Tanzania, the tallest free standing mountain in the world. It stands at 5,895metres above sea level. This mountain is the closest to the equator, which means that when I was on the summit, I was the fastest moving stationary object on the planet. I had received an email in July of 2008 asking for Vision impaired people who were prepared to participate in a 'Determination Walk' to volunteer, and this adventure was to include our own fundraising. Who knew how this would change my current life?

Fundraising is the most difficult, frustrating and draining experience I have had on the phone. When signing on the dotted line, I had no idea of the difficulty of moving forward and raising the monies required for such a trek. Calling people on the phone is the easy part. Letting them know what I am doing is also rewarding. Most of the persons I contacted were complimentary on how much of an inspiration I am. Fantastic, hand over the cash! At least with the phone calls I was able to filter out the persons who were not so flattering, bringing my database down to a level of people who were really interested in what I was doing.

During the days leading up to the day of packing and leaving, I went through so many different emotions, fear being one of them. This was to be the first time I had ever been out of Australia. I did not have fear of losing my life, just the fear of trusting my surroundings to someone else. At home I am able to control my environment, whether it is food, clothing danger, or tripping over something, or making sure things are placed for me to quickly and easily find them. I like to have order because knowing where anything is, when I need it, is very important to me and so it should be, as I just don't have sight! The frustration of residing with someone, be it for a short time, knowing that how they live at home is nowhere near as tidy as I do, did factor in my fear, or is that anxiety?

Each person, sighted and vision impaired, on the trek was told they should use a hiking pole. This pole had a point at the end. I felt this would be a hindrance for me. I chose to use a white cane with a large rolling ball. This was most useful as the track we were to walk along was rough. With the larger ball I was able to navigate around the larger rocks or locate the gutters that were dug out for guiding the water to cross the track.

Not everybody makes it to the top. For example, the night after we attempted and succeeded in reaching the summit, a couple ascended to approximately 5,100 metres, started throwing up, so turned around. From what I understand once you turn around that's the end of that attempt. We were so fortunate to have twenty-five climbers achieve Gillman's Point, and have twenty-four of those continue to Uhuru.

One of the quotes I use sometimes is; 'You can plan but you can't predict.' In saying that, I am not sure what my future will bring, but I'm sure it will be great.

I have a new challenge to achieve and am researching what it is right now - Fundraising for the Prevent Blindness Foundation.

I also run my own company called 'Very Important Phone Calls'

Statistics have shown that email campaigns may have a 6% click through. Where mail out campaigns may have a 2% return. VIPAS, my company, can guarantee an 87-94% response to a telephone campaign.

You provide the contact list. I conduct the telephone campaign confidentially, on your behalf for your reasons. I then return the spreadsheet with any comments and queries your clients may have.

Perhaps you'd like to take a look at these sites.

www.everydayhero.com.au/brian_haupt

and my business site;

www.vipas.biz

JALEESA – SURVIVES AND THRIVES – SHE JUST LIVES!

BY JALEESA PON

Hi there, I'm Jaleesa Pon.

Just to give you a bit of background on who I am… I'm nineteen and I live in Brisbane, Australia. I love the arts; I play piano, sing and dance. I love going to the theatre and travelling overseas. I have many goals and big dreams that I want to achieve in life, one being to make a difference in the world.

I'd love to say that I have an amazing story, one where I've overcome huge obstacles to accomplish all the things I have to date, because those kinds of stories always seem more interesting and believable, but the fact is I don't. I'm just a person who is passionate about making sure people don't give up on themselves and I'm someone who wants to see other people living a full and happy life – a life where people are taking chances on themselves and their possibilities… where people are daring to live!

Too often I see people who have big dreams and aspirations, dreams and aspirations that are quite achievable, give up on themselves. Why? People do this for a number of different reasons. It could be that:

they're afraid of failing;

they're scared of what other people might think of them and their judgments and criticisms;

they're scared of their own success, they're not sure of what life might look like when they go ahead and achieve great things; or

they might feel unworthy so never give their hopes and dreams a chance.

Now, I admit, I was once this kind of person – I was content to live a reasonable life because I was absolutely petrified of what other people would think of me if I did 'this' or 'that' and I was 110% terrified of failing and looking bad to others.

To this day, I still have my reservations; I have moments when the doubt creeps in and the fear of what people will think of me if I fail pops up… and these times are really scary because I find myself at a cross roads, trying to figure out whether I should 'go for it' or not.

Then, the strangest thing happens to me… Just when I'm about to give up on myself and my dreams, the doubtful voice in my head changes and starts to say things like:

"How will I feel if I don't do this?"

"What will my life look like in ten years time if I give up on this now?"

"Will I be where I truly want to be?"

"Will I be happy and content or will I be bitter and regretful?"

Just when I'm about to 'throw in the towel', I start to dare… I dare to dream and I dare to believe in myself and what I am capable of doing.

One such moment where I found myself at 'the cross roads', was only last year after I broke up with my boyfriend of three years. Now you might be reading this and thinking, "here we go… another tragic love story…" but you're wrong… It wasn't a tragic love story; it was actually a gift in disguise.

Okay, so yeah, I was pretty messed up! Actually, that's an understatement… I was pretty hysterical! At the time I felt like my heart had been ripped out of my chest and I thought the sky was going to fall and my entire world was going to end (I'm not making this more dramatic for the sake of a good story… I was a major drama queen!). My whole world had been tipped upside down! I mean, I was eighteen years-old and I was no longer with the 'love of my life' nor was I going to live happily ever after. (I'll make my point now and save you from all the theatrics!)

Basically, I was lost. How I thought my life would turn out and the plans I had made for myself and those around me no longer applied or existed.

So there I was, eighteen years-old, lost and at a cross roads. I found myself sitting by the bay in my car one day balling my eyes out – wondering what I was supposed to do with myself now. Then (like it happens in the movies), I felt a light bulb go off in my head!

In this moment I realised that I was not alone. I was not the only person in the world who felt heartbreak and experienced all these different emotions. I thought of my friends and saw how they too had to deal with a lot of internal and external pressures and how even though we may all come from different places and have different life experiences, fundamentally we're all the same – we're complex human beings.

After realising this, I came up with the idea of Positive Teen Talk and found purpose in my life again and discovered what I really want to do with my life and how I want to contribute to the happiness and success of other people and the world around us. I thought, "It would be great for teens to share their stories with each other! How great would it be to allow others to learn from each others' experiences and create an encouraging, supportive and positive community?"

So with only a little bit of money in my bank account and a lot of faith, I created an online community and mentoring program for teenagers called Positive Teen Talk (www.positiveteentalk.com). Positive Teen Talk is all about *Happy Teens, Worldly Dreams* and our mission is to help teenagers build strong personal foundations for themselves (healthy self-esteem, confidence and self-love) so that they can feel confident in themselves and their abilities. I believe that when people are happy, they become excited about life and its possibilities and that's what PTT is all about – showing teens how they can lead happy, healthy, successful and fulfilling lives.

I say, "let us make an impact on the teens of today so we can help them create successes for their tomorrows."

Now don't get the impression that I did all of this 'just like that'… There were MANY times when I wanted to call it quits and give up! Times when I didn't feel that anything was working and I felt like I was all alone in my quest for happiness for myself and for teens. But it was in these moments, times when I felt like everything was going to fall apart and when I was on the verge of breaking down, that I actually had breakthroughs and the greatest success.

The past year has been the biggest and scariest rollercoaster of my life! I've experienced extreme highs but also the deepest of lows, and I've found out that all I need to do to be successful for myself is bet on me!

Please don't get the impression that I'm a gambler… I can barely play poker! What I mean is that I've learnt how to bet on myself and take chances… calculated risks… and I've learnt how to succeed at doing this!

Now, my secret recipe is actually pretty simple. When there's something that I really want to do or achieve, all I do is this… I cook up a dare and I add it to my dream or goal, a dash of belief and a plan of action and Voilà! The result is a perfect recipe for success. You can do and be absolutely anything that you want to be. All you have to do is dare to be your possibilities.

The opportunities available to you and what you can do with your life are boundless... In fact, your possibilities are infinite! This is something that I've learnt over the past few years and I know it to be true because I have experienced the results of 'daring' and 'betting on me' in my own life…

All you have to do is believe in yourself and in your dreams! Faith is a mover of mountains. All you have to do is bet on yourself and take the plunge. You'll be surprised at how successful you'll be when you bet on yourself and dare to live.

Believe in yourself and in your dreams because you're worth it!

All the best,

Jaleesa Pon

Positive Teen Talk

"Happy Teens, Worldly Dreams"

If you'd like to learn more about Positive Teen Talk and what Jaleesa is doing, feel free to visit Positive Teen Talk's website

www.positiveteentalk.com.

THEY DARED

There you have seven very different stories from seven very different people with seven different backgrounds and seven different challenges. They all turned their challenges into opportunities and went onwards and upwards. The reason they were able to do this was, because and in spite of the obstacles put in their way, each one developed a positive attitude and mindset energy to set their lives on a wonderful path of discovery and achievement.

Each person looked at what had happened in the past and learnt something valuable from it. They did something different to make their lives what they are now. They are all focussed on what is right for them now and respond to what is important for them now.

They all have plans and dreams for the future and are taking actions to help make them happen. They are wonderful, motivated people who have shown that *we can be and do anything we want to if we only want it badly enough.* They dared to live. Do you dare? Trust yourself!

ABOUT THE AUTHOR

Born in London in 1946. Diane emigrated with her family to the then country of Rhodesia at the age of ten. Schooled at Lord Malvern and studied at the Teachers' College, Bulawayo, she spent almost all her professional life in education, ending up as Deputy Head at Hillcrest Preparatory School, Mutare and then as Head of Mvurachena School in Chipinge in Zimbabwe.

She looks at herself as a survivor and thriver. She has led an exciting and varied life on four continents, experiencing many adventures that others would find extremely daunting. She has canoed on the Zambesi River, been on Safari in Africa, crossed the Tanami Desert, raced saloon cars, climbed glaciers, was an instructor at Outward Bound, swum with dolphins, been deep sea diving, climbed the Chimanimani Mountains, arrested in Mexico, married and brought up two children.

Over the last few years, she has survived a wild animal attack and the subsequent operations to put her back together again, has lived with tyrannical persecution within the oppressive Zimbabwean regime, coping with political harassment, brutality and bullying by Mugabe's henchmen. She followed her heart and 'eloped' with her first love, whom she hadn't seen for over forty years. She handled the deaths of her first husband, elder daughter and mother, all within a few weeks of each other, with fortitude.

Diane puts her indomitable spirit down to her very positive attitude, and since her retirement from her position as school principal of a Private School in Zimbabwe, at the end of 2006, has tried to spread the message of *Mindset Energy*, the power of positive thinking and positive attitude, to anyone and everyone she can reach. She believes that you can be and do anything you want to, if you really want it badly enough. You just have to have the right *Mindset Energy*.

Diane is now a professional speaker, a speaker with a difference. Using real-life stories, Diane weaves her message, engaging and entertaining her audiences.

Showing you how to use –

Mindset Energy - the attitude to propel your life and your business forward!

Contact Diane: diane.inoz@bigpond.com

www.ingramcontent.com/pod-product-compliance
Lightning Source LLC
LaVergne TN
LVHW020638100826
845148LV00012B/2233